Please remember that this is a library book,
and that it belongs only temporarily to each
person who uses it. Be considerate. Do
not write in this, or any, library book.

WITHDRAWN

Dreams in the Psychology of Religion

Dreams in the Psychology of Religion

James Gollnick

Volume 1
Studies in the Psychology of Religion

The Edwin Mellen Press
Lewiston/Queenston

Library of Congress Cataloging-in-Publication Data

Gollnick, James.
  Dreams in the psychology of religion.

  Studies in the psychology of religion ; v. 1.
  Bibliography: p.
  Includes index.
  1. Dreams. 2. Psychology, Religious. I. Title. II. Series:
Studies in the psychology of religion (Edwin Mellen Press) ; v. 1.
BF 1078.G47 1987 200'.1'9   87-18539
ISBN 0-88946-248-8

This is volume 1 in the continuing series
Studies in the Psychology of Religion
Volume 1 ISBN 0-88946-248-8
SPR Series ISBN 0-88946-247-X

The Edwin Mellen Press   The Edwin Mellen Press
P.O. Box 450   P.O. Box 67
Lewiston, New York   Queenston, Ontario
USA 14092   CANADA L0S 1L0

Printed in the United States of America

*To My Brothers,
Albert and John,
and their families*

Acknowledgements

I wish to thank David Seljak, Eda Soudant, and Professors Herbert Richardson, Peter Beyer and Bruce Alton, for their assistance in preparing this book.

I would also like to thank Muriel Kinney and Professors Lawrence Elmer, Roger Hutchinson and William Callahan of the University of Toronto for their interest and encouragement in this project.

Table of Contents

Introduction

In this book I wish to describe the theory and practice of dream interpretation in the psychology of religion. The psychology of religion is a very broad subject and dream interpretation is but a small subset of the whole field.[1] Often it is hard to tell who is working in this area since the people involved are found in various contexts such as psychotherapy, psychoanalysis, experimental psychology, humanistic psychology and transpersonal psychology. For our purposes we shall include anyone working on dreams who has an attitude open to religious interpretations.

My own work on dream interpretation has taken place primarily in two settings, the academic and the therapeutic. In the academic setting we distinguish between the "objective" study about dreams and the therapeutic use of dreams. Of course there is often some overlapping here since even a non-clinical interest in our own dreams may turn out to be therapeutic. In undergraduate courses at the University of Toronto we do not practice dream analysis except by way of illustration, though students are invited to apply some of the theoretical principles of dream interpretation to their own dreams in the form of research papers or seminar presentations. This course work is distinct from the extracurricular dream seminars or groups I run as a voluntary activity and which are illustrated in chapter four.

In the extracurricular seminars we have developed a method of dream interpretation that takes into account the contributions of the major forces of psychology and considers the religious interpretation of dreams. As you will see in the illustration of group dream work these voluntary seminars are much more personally involving than academic courses. We practice dream interpretation here not as a therapeutic or clinical technique but as an art that enriches life. Again, as in the academic courses, this work may have a therapeutic effect on the participants but psychotherapy is not the aim of these seminars.

At the Gestalt Institute of Toronto I have been involved in dream seminars in a therapeutic setting. There we explore how Gestalt as well as other psychological approaches contribute to dream interpretation. Jorge Rosner, director of the Gestalt Institute, has long been an innovator in humanistic psychology and has enthusiastically supported these dream seminars. Since my overriding interest remains the psychology of religion, I employ the method described in chapter three even in the therapeutic settings of the Gestalt Institute and my private practice.

As both Freud and Jung advised long ago, personal conviction based on work with your own dreams is essential for understanding the meaning of dreams. I think you will also find this to be true if you try out for yourself some of the rules of dream interpretation described in this book. Over the last fifteen years I have tested Freud's advice by recording, analyzing and contemplating over 3,000 of my own dreams. That experience guides my approach to this book.

In the first three chapters I shall discuss dreams in history, psychology and the psychology of religion. Chapter one describes both the religious origins and recent developments of dream interpretation. The recent trends may be summarized as a move toward more democratic and participatory dream interpretation. Chapter two shows how the major forces of psychology have contributed to methods of dream interpretation and chapter three situates dream interpretation in the psychology of religion. For those primarily interested in the practice of interpreting dreams I would suggest moving directly from chapter one to chapter four, the practical application.

This final chapter examines the rules for interpreting dreams and provides an illustration of how these rules are applied in a dream group. These rules for interpreting dreams involve the debate between religion and science. I hope to show that those who exclude the possibility of a religious interpretation of dreams do so not on scientific (empirical) grounds but on the basis of philosophical (materialist and reductionist) presuppositions.

In my rules for dream interpretation I hope to point to the spiritual potential of dreams without imposing religious interpretations on dream material. Those who would explore the way of dreams as a possible spiritual path will find some historical and psychological orientation and precedent in these pages. This method has proved to be effective in both group and individual dream interpretation and I hope the reader will benefit from working with dreams in some of the ways suggested here.

Note

1. The psychology of religion involves the psychological analysis of various dimensions of religion such as religious experience, doctrine, myth, ritual, community, ethics, spiritual healing and human transformation. Dreams have an important place in this field because nearly all the major religions of the world have considered dreams as a principal means of divine revelation and some have considered them as potential forms of mystical experience (See M. Kelsey, *God, Dreams and Revelation* (Minneapolis, 1974), p. 1). The psychological investigation of religion may focus on any religion and may be carried out from the perspective of any of the major forces of psychology discussed in chapter two.

Chapter I

Dream Interpretation
in Historical Perspective

I shall not attempt to cover the entire history of dream interpretation here, but merely indicate certain developments in
history that shed light on the present state of the art. The
earliest approaches to dreams considered them as a part of a
religious world view. Dreams were thought to be messages from
the gods or actual visitations by the gods or the spirits.[1] In
dreams the gods might advise a course of action or warn about
some present or future danger. The ancients tried to make sense
of these dreams not as signs of a person's psychological life, but
as real experiences in which the dreamer encounters the gods or
disembodied souls.

Different cultures evaluated the dreamer's relationship to
the gods or spirits differently. The Babylonians and Assyrians,
for example, considered bad dreams to be caused by devils and
spirits of the dead. These dream demons were to be warded off
and if they did enter a dream, magical practices were necessary
to cast them out of the dreamer's life.[2] The Egyptians saw
dreams primarily as supernatural messages sent from the gods.
The Egyptian dream interpreters were called "The Learned Men
of the Magic Library" and they often lived secluded in temples
where people came to dream and have their dreams interpreted.
The Egyptians recognized three categories of dreams: 1) where
the gods demand something of humans, such as repentance; 2)

where the gods warn of dangers ahead; and 3) where the gods give answers to the dreamer's questions.[3] In each case dreams are considered as a vehicle for communicating with the gods.

The Egyptian dream temples dedicated to Serapis, the God of dreams, were monuments to the religious interpretation of dreams. People seeking help for illness or some other problem would come to these temples to fast and pray. Then they would fall asleep in the holy place so that the gods might cure or answer them directly in the dream or communicate to them how a cure or answer could be found. The temple priests were available to interpret these dreams and to assist in cures recommended in the dream.

This process of going to a holy place to receive a dream in answer to a problem or illness is called dream incubation.[4] This practice was not restricted to Egypt but spread throughout the ancient world so that there were hundreds of active dream temples thorughout Greece and the Roman Empire.[5]

The Greeks developed this art to a high degree and dedicated their temples to Aesculapius, the god of medicine. In these temples, people would pray and then sleep in order to be healed by the god Aesculapius himself or to receive instruction about what medicine to administer or what action to take in order to be healed. Again, as in the Egyptian dream temples, interpreters would be on hand to interpret the incubated dream and specify the appropriate treatment when it was not clearly spelled out in the dream.

From the widespread, institutionalized practice of dream incubation we can see how much attention was given to dreams in the ancient world and how dreams were intimately related to beliefs about the gods and the spirits. In this ancient context of dream interpretation people assumed that if a god appeared in a dream, the dreamer actually experienced the presence of that god.

Judaism and Christianity carried on this ancient sensitivity to the religious nature of dreams.[6] In these traditions the dream still provided an arena of divine-human contact. Now however, the one God, Yahweh, and not the many gods, was thought to be the source of all good dreams. God continued to reveal himself in dreams and often guided his people in this way.[7] Dreams were, in this tradition, potentially the voice of God. There are in the Bible however, many passages expressing caution about dreams and dream interpreters. While dreams were considered a primary method of divine revelation, some dreams were thought to be from demons, so careful discernment was required to distinguish between good and evil dreams.

Other cultures also followed this almost universal tendency to interpret dreams within a religious world view. In ancient China the source of dreams was considered to be the spiritual soul which can separate from the body and thereby communicate with spirits or souls of the dead during dreams.[8] Even though the gods are not seen here as the source of dreams, dreams are still considered in a religious light, that is, the soul is thought to be actually encountering the spirits or the souls of the dead. So the dream images of the spirits are considered as the actual presence of the spirits symbolized.

In India dreams were also considered from a religious point of view. The Vedas, the sacred books of ancient India, discuss the favorable or unfavorable meanings of certain dream symbols.[9] A major concern of East Indian thinking on dreams has to do with the different levels of reality (such as waking, sleeping, dreaming, visions, and meditation) and where the reality of dreams fits on this scale.[10] Dreaming is considered an intermediate state between this world and the spiritual world. From the dream state one can see both of these worlds at the same time.[11] This represents another way of tackling the fundamental question of whether dream images of the gods, spirits or souls of the dead are strictly in the mind of the dreamer or actually evoke the presence of these spiritual phenomena themselves.

In this tradition dreams also implied a path to enlightenment. In the Upanishads, for example, the reality of dreams was considered as one of four states of being: waking, dreaming, dreamless sleep and the supernatural state of identity with the Godhead. This analysis of the four states leads to a technique of self-realization. If a person understands that he is actually dreaming when he thinks he is awake, he can begin to realize that there is a further state of awakening that is the fourth state of being, the transcendent state of identity with God.[12] So here, too, the spiritual possibilities of dreams are highlighted.

In the geographical areas influenced by Islam there was also great emphasis on the religious potential of dreams. The very foundations of Islam are tied to dream revelation in that it is based on the Qu'ran, much of which was revealed to Mohammed by the angel Gabriel in dreams. A noted scholar of Islam has stated that there is hardly a phase of life in Islam where dreams do not play a part and this intense concern with dreams is within a religious context.[13]

There is a religious context for dream interpretation not only in the cultures influenced by the major world religions, but in various other cultures as well. Among many African tribes dreams are viewed from a religious perspective as a potential mode of communication with the dead and superior powers.[14] Dreams are also a way to get information about the identity of sorcerers and the future. For the Ashanti of the Gold Coast dreams are thought to be visitations from the spirit world or the journey of the dreamer's own soul.[15]

Many North American Indian tribes also deal with dreams in terms of a religious world view. The Hopi Indians stress the importance of dreams and many of their dreams contain images of the gods.[16] The Ojibway Indians also rely heavily on a religious interpretation of dreams. The "dream visitors" are familiar "other-than-human" entities which play a significant role in Ojibway society, especially during the "dream fast." In the dream fast boys between the ages of ten and fifteen are sent out to fast for six or seven nights.[17] This is designed to provoke pity from the other-than-human grandfather so they may send a dream vision.

Blessings, powers, songs and new moral obligations come from the visions of the dream fast. Ojibway boys also hope to receive a vocation (such as conjurer or medicine man) and life instructions during the dream fast. The Crow, Menomeni, Winnebago, Sioux and other Indian tribes also stress the importance of a dream fast or vision quest as the crucial social event in tribal life. In these cultures the dream is an arena where humans

meet the spirits or the gods and often the impact of this encounter affects the dreamer's entire life. The religious dream
figures here are seen as the actual spiritual realities they
symbolize.

A central question emerges in this brief overview of
historical and cultural attitudes toward dreams: What is the
status of dream reality? Is the dream less real, equally real or
more real than waking life? It is clear from some of the examples of dream interpretation within a religious context that
the status of dreams and dream figures is given a high accent of
reality. In sharp contrast to the widespread contemporary viewpoint that dreams are unreal and meaningless, the Yuma and
Mohave Indians believe that dreaming is more real than waking.
For the Yuma Indians whatever is dreamed has already happened or is about to happen. For the Mohave Indians the dream
not only has greater reality than waking life, it also controls
waking life by guiding what is thought and done.[18]

However, even in the ancient world there were some who
did not believe that dreams were the door to the world of the
gods and spirits. the most influential figure in this regard was
Aristotle. He rejected the theory that dreams were sent from the
gods.[19] If the gods were the source of dreams, he argued, they
would send dreams only to the wisest and most rational people.
But since dreams occur even to ignorant and irrational people,
the gods are not the authors of our dreams.

With this line of reasoning Aristotle replaced the divine
origin of dreams with the theory that dreams are merely the impressions left over from sense activity. According to this view
external stimuli are reduced during sleep so attention can be
focused on internal sensations which may reveal physical disturbances that have not yet manifested themselves. So while
dreams were no longer considered by Aristotle to be divine, they
still retained some value for physicians who could use them for
diagnosis. Cicero was another major figure in the ancient world
who denied that dreams come from God. In fact Cicero went
even further to say that dreams do not deserve any credit or
respect at all. He advocated that dream interpretation should be
rejected because it was a superstition that oppressed the intellect

and led people into believing silly things.[20]

In the medieval period there were forces at work which carried on this critical view of dreams. Morton Kelsey, who has studied the history of dream interpretation extensively, sees the powerful influence of St. Thomas Aquinas as a primary reason why the Christian Church ceased to value dreams as it had in its early centuries.[21] St. Thomas was influenced by Aristotle's negative judgment about the possibility of divine dreams. This led to a neglect of dreams and their religious significance. Kelsey also maintains that the Church tended to view religious dreams with suspicion since these dreams threatened the Church's position as sole mediator with God.

These are some of the factors that led to a shift in the value placed on dreams and especially the religious significance of dreams by the end of the Middle Ages. There was also a general shift to the view that dreams were either meaningless, occult, or merely derived from external or internal stimuli. The Age of Reason and the rise of a scientific world view further supported this trend toward devaluing dreams.[22] The broad historical movement called Romanticism, a reaction to the Enlightenment's emphasis on reason and society, briefly countered this generally negative evaluation of dreams.

The Romantics spoke of communication with another reality, more vast, prior and superior to the individual life. Romantic writers gave a privileged place to the dream. For example, Karl-Philipp Moritz saw dreams as symbols of the existence of an ideal world and reminiscences of states prior to the separated consciousness we experience as distinct individuals. This theme is also found in C.G. Carus and Schopenhauer. Moritz also spoke of the night as the guardian of treasures and dreams as a mystical language.[23] For C.G. Carus, the unconscious is the subjective expression of nature, the relative unconscious is distinct from the absolute unconscious and dreams can unveil a supra-individual reality. These ideas have a striking resemblance to Carl Jung's view of the unconscious as a product of nature and his distinction between the personal and collective unconscious.

Novalis saw dreams as revelations of a secret and magical

world.[24] E.T. Hoffmann considered dreams as a gate through which divine messages come and he said that the "god of dreams" dictated to him his most dramatic works.[25] Gerard de Nerval called the dream a "second life," an opening to the invisible world of the spirits.[26] Victor Hugo reached back to the earliest recorded view of dreams as the place where God is revealed to men and Charles Baudelaire thought that some dreams could reveal the supernatural side of life. Charles Nodier spoke of dreams as a rite of passage enabling him to communicate with the dead and past civilizations and to know future events.[27] While the Romantics experienced revelations and magic in dreams they realized that the journey to the land of dreams could also be a perilous adventure. Arthur Rimbaud encountered dissociation of the ego in his dream journey and Stephane Mallarme described moments of madness interspersed with ecstacy and losing contact with reality.[28]

After the brief renaissance of Romantic dream appreciation in the early part of the 19th century, the era of positivism again asserted that dreams are meaningless. The positivists maintained that dreams are the by-product of automatic and unco-ordinated brain activity during sleep.[29] This was the climate of opinion when Freud published his ground-breaking study, *The Interpretation of Dreams.* Freud's discoveries about dreams grew out of his medical practice. Some of his patients would mention their dreams while speaking of their symptoms. He observed how certain sexual and aggressive impulses in his patients played a large role in their dreams. Freud interpreted these impulses as wishes which were unknown to, or at least unacknowledged by, the dreamer. He also noticed that these wishes were often connected to the symptoms that brought the person to seek treatment. He found that often when a patient became aware of these wishes that the symptoms associated with them disappeared.

Freud's genius was to take dreams seriously again, as the ancients and various religious traditions had done. For Freud, and for all dream analysts since, the most important single assumption in dream interpretation is that dreams are meaningful. Without this initial presupposition people would, and many still do, dismiss dreams as meaningless, as products of haphazard processes. Without the initial confidence that dreams are valuable and do have meaning, we do not take the time required to make sense of dream symbols. Attention, and even detective work, is necessary in order to understand the plot of a dream and the significance of dream figures and their actions. As Freud indicated, the meaning of a dream symbol usually becomes clear only after sifting through a variety of feelings, thoughts and memories associated with that symbol. Initial confidence in the meaning and value of dreams is only confirmed as the various elements of a dream begin to fall into place.

After Freud's crucial step of insisting that dreams are meaningful, he proceeded to describe the meaning that he found. The many examples we have from *The Interpretation of Dreams* show what an astute observer Freud was. He noticed particularly how dream themes of sex and aggression are related to the dreamer's waking experience. But Freud did not pay sufficient attention to elements other than sex and aggression that also appear in dreams.

Freud's psychoanalysis placed great emphasis on the analyst's interpretations of the patient's dreams and mental life. This developed a model of dream interpretation that made the analyst the authority on the meaning of the patient's dreams. This represented a return to a kind of authoritative dream interpretation reminiscent of the ancients, only now it was no longer carried on in the domain of dream temples under the aura of gods and religion. The consulting room replaced the dream temple, but the authoritative position of the psychoanalyst was similar to the ancient dream interpreter.

Psychoanalysis is not unique in this "analyst as authority" model of dream interpretation. Other schools largely followed this psychoanalytic model with various modifications. While particular dream interpretations differed from school to school, the authoritative position of the analyst was largely unquestioned. But two shifts have gradually occurred in the course of the twentieth century: 1) Various interpreters have presented coherent and often equally plausible alternative interpretations of dreams and 2) methods in psychology have moved away from the "analyst as authority" model to the "dreamer as the authority" model. I shall say a few words about both of these developments.

After Freud, other observers who did not have the same exclusive commitment to sex and aggression as the mainsprings of human life were able to give fuller value to other aspects of dreams. Carl Jung, for instance, emphasized mythological and religious symbols in dreams. While he began his career interpreting these symbols reductively as Freud had done, Jung later considered religious elements to be fundamental to human life and not simply projections of the dreamer's personal psychology.[30] Erich Fromm, Erik Erikson and others also broadened the range of dream elements described by analysts.[31] They placed more emphasis on the dynamics of interpersonal relationships and the social aspects of human life that appear in dreams. In chapter four I shall deal with some of the consequences of recognizing multiple, alternative interpretations of dream symbols.

The other major twentieth-century development in dream interpretation is to transfer the authority regarding the meaning of dreams from the analyst to the dreamer. This move is related to larger developments in humanistic psychology where much therapeutic work involves clients in resolving their own problems and helps make them more aware of their own participation in their illness and health. Shifting the authority in dream interpretation from the analyst back to the dreamer gives increased attention to the role of dreams outside the clinical setting. This development may be thought of as "democratizing" dream interpretation because it emphasizes the ability of ordinary dreamers to understand their own dreams without necessarily relying on professional analysts or therapists. There are a number of works in recent years that reflect this movement. Here I would like to discuss just a few of the more important books that contribute to this widening appreciation of dreams.

Ann Faraday's popular work, *The Dream Game*, draws upon her long experience both in the laboratory investigation of dreams and in various forms of psychotherapy, including Freudian analysis, Jungian analysis and Gestalt therapy. Dr. Faraday emphasizes that most people do not need expert help to understand their dreams and that dreams express in the "language of the heart" people's deep feelings about their present life. From her work with clients and friends she offers many examples of how dreams portray our current life experience in a dramatic fashion that often sheds new light on the meaning of that experience. She shows how dreams often place our life situation in a different light, revealing new dimensions of interest and excitement that were previously hidden. Interpersonal relationships are frequently presented in ways that show new possibilities or flaws that might have been hidden from awareness. Thus dreams provide an alternative point of view that can suggest improvements in a relationship and a way out of an impasse.

Faraday underscores the "objective" dimensions of dreams in her work. This means that as she reflects on the meaning of a dream, she considers the possibility that the dream may be commenting on some actual situation in the external world. She offers the example of having a disturbing dream shortly after moving into a new apartment on the seventh floor.[32] Her dream showed her falling off the balcony. The next morning she examined the guardrails on the balcony and found that they were in fact rickety and unsafe. Quite possibly she had noticed this dangerous state of affairs at a subliminal level and this information reached her awareness only at the moment of the dream. From her experience with such dreams she recognizes the value of checking whether a dream might be offering valuable information about people and situations in the external world. Faraday refers to this helpful role of dreams as the "watchdogs of the psyche."

Faraday's approach recognizes and appreciates a variety of dimensions in dreams, that is, the many different types of experience dreams comment on. She also emphasizes the ability of non-experts to understand something about their own dreams since the dream is a picture language that most people can learn once they realize the simplicity and directness of this language.

Her work opens the way to the use of dreams by people who simply desire greater self knowledge and a keener awareness of the world around them whether or not they are in psychotherapy.

Montague Ullman and Nan Zimmerman present many practical suggestions in *Working With Dreams*. Their work is designed to aid non-experts in understanding dreams. They presuppose that dreams are essentially subjective since they maintain that the goal of dream analysis is to reclaim aspects of ourselves that we have neglected or disowned.[33] They state that joy, excitement and hope are some of the rewards for spending time with our own dreams. According to Ullman and Zimmerman dreams reveal who we really are, that is, our actual psychological state. Their view tends toward a completely subjective interpretation of dream figures and images: they say that all dreams are problem solving or attempts at solutions.[34] This tends to reduce the potential import of dreams to a single function, namely, dealing with the dreamer's problems. While they are aware that in earlier times people believed dreams could manifest the divine will or the spirit world, they attribute this belief to a pre-scientific mentality.

Ullman does acknowledge telepathy and altered states of consciousness in dreams although he does not explicitly coordinate this position with his view that dreams reveal the dreamer's inner self. Ullman's investigation of telepathy broadens his otherwise exclusively subjective interest in dreams.

The authors state that most people do not need expert help in order to understand their dreams.[35] They advocate group work as the best way for many people to understand their dreams because 1) the group can offer emotional support as we try to discover insights provided by our dreams and 2) other people frequently read our dream metaphors better than we do since they do not have to deal with the consequences of these insights. They also contribute to "democratizing" dream interpretation when they maintain that dream work is often effective outside a clinical setting and need not be guided by a professional.

Strephon Williams' *Jungian-Senoi Dreamwork Manual* is

designed as a guide for do-it-yourself dreamwork. He prefers to speak of actualizing rather than interpreting dreams.[36] By actualizing a dream Williams means reexperiencing it, getting closer to the dream through a series of exercises designed to bring the dream alive and reveal the implications of the dream for the dreamer's waking life and environment. To actualize a dream, for example, he may draw or paint a dream symbol, or try out new behavior that was pictured in a dream. Dream actualization especially involves recapturing the emotional intensity of dreams and doing specific outer-life projects inspired by dreams. For Williams actualizing a dream is more immediate and emotionally involving than interpreting it. He rejects dream "interpretation" because for him it means translating dream images into concepts and fitting specific living symbols into generalized conceptual systems.

Williams is especially sensitive to the ever-present danger of the analyst's projections contaminating dream interpretation.[37] Interpretation often means that the analyst takes over another person's dream by calling on mythology or some psychological theory to tell dreamers what their dream symbols mean. The problem with this kind of interpretation is that dreamers are not sufficiently involved in their own process of discovery but instead are told what to think about their dreams.

Williams encourages people to work on their own dreams and frequently reminds us that dreamers are the ultimate authority over their own dreams. He describes a variety of dreamwork techniques designed for individual and group use. Williams recognizes that some of his methods are derived from Jungian and Gestalt psychology, such as the Jungian technique of active imagination for observing any changes or development in dream symbols or the Gestalt technique for identifying with and enacting each of the dream symbols.[38] He also presents other techniques to guide people in exploring their own dreams and thus contributes effectively to democratizing dream interpretation.

Williams describes techniques that are valuable for discovering not only the subjective, psychological meanings of dreams but also the objective, outer-world and spiritual levels of meaning. He and his dream groups consider the role of dreams in developing the spiritual life by asking such questions as where does my dream come from and where does it lead me? He also uses dreams to explore psychic awareness (precognitive and telepathic dreams), lucid dreams (where a person is aware of being in a dream while dreaming) and synchronicity (meaningful coincidences between dream symbols and outer life).

Dick McLeester's *Welcome to the Magic Theater* represents another step in democratizing the dream. His book is essentially an annotated bibliography along with some perceptive observations about dream interpretation. McLeester himself prefers to speak of "working on" dreams rather than analyzing or interpreting them.[39] His book provides a good overview of the field and is a helpful introduction to dream interpretation. McLeester emphasizes that dreamwork should lead to action in our lives. He sees the benefits of dreamwork being not so much intellectual insights as the power to change the dreamer's life in some way.[40] To achieve this he suggests that after working on a dream, the dreamer should sum up what she has learned and how she intends to act on this new knowledge.

While dreams most frequently reflect our preoccupations, attitudes and feelings, they also deal with the world around us. For McLeester dreams bring together both the personal and social worlds. From this vantage point dreamwork is a vehicle for social change. To understand dreams at this level we must learn to recognize the social world and the environment in the images of our dreams and to ask how a particular dream relates to the world and our interaction with it. Another dimension of dreams that McLeester attends to is the spiritual. He notes that dreams frequently reflect our religious beliefs, generate religious experiences and reveal the spiritual depths of everyday life. McLeester suggests that working with dreams may complement whatever spiritual path we are following. As in so many areas of life, dreams may provide us with valuable insights about our religious experience, institutions and values.

Richard Jones' book *The Dream Poet* provides a lively account of his "Dream Reflection Seminars." The goal of these seminars is to enjoy, appreciate and learn from dreams.[41] This represents a shift away from the analytic posture which focuses on correct interpretation and exposing personal conflict. In the Humanities classroom, dreams provide a very personal knowledge of a subject and they often reveal deep feelings about a topic whether it be a poem, an artifact or a broad cultural pattern.

Jones highlights the capacity of dreams to reveal positive elements of the personality. Although his orientation is Freudian, he differs with Freud on the meaning of dreams. Where Freud sees dreams as analogous to neurotic symptoms, Jones compares them to artistic visions that unlock new ways of looking at life and problems.[42] Where Freud focuses on the objectivity of the analyst's interpretation, Jones concentrates on the subjectivity of the dreamer's feelings and intuition. The ultimate authority in dream reflection is the dreamer according to Jones.

John Sanford's *Dreams, God's Forgotten Language* is another work that supports democratizing dream interpretation, in this case from a Jungian perspective. Sanford is an Episcopalean priest who argues convincingly for a religious interpretation of dreams. When dealing with dreams, psychology and religion are inseparable, according to Sanford. He focuses particularly on the religious meanings that are played out in dreams. He demonstrates this in his approach to the Shadow, a Jungian concept that represents negative and underdeveloped aspects of the personality. He maintains that the Shadow is not just a psychological problem, but also a religious struggle.[43]

Dreams show inner conflicts that have spiritual significance, though the symbols representing these spiritual conflicts may or may not have any obvious connection to traditional religious symbols. At this level religion has to do with the meaning of life and ethical values acted out in our lives whether or not they are symbolized in religious terms. In Sanford's view the meaning of life, the integration of personality and the commitment to ethical values are all essentially religious concerns. Sanford's interest in the religious meaning of dreams leads him to recognize that dream interpretation is not the exclusive domain of psychology. He favors the view that ordinary people (non-experts) should attend to their dreams since they can find in them a place where God contacts human beings.

Morton Kelsey, also an Episcopalean priest, argues even more forcefully than Sanford for attention to dreams as a way to develop spirituality. Kelsey, in *God, Dreams and Revelation*, raises the question of why Christians have such little interest in dreams when all the major religions of the world have considered them valuable avenues of religious experience. He points out that religious people have turned to their dreams for a variety of reasons such as learning about things to come, guidance from God and the spirits or experiencing God. His study is essentially historical. I have already mentioned two of the reasons he cites why the Church's early interest in dreams vanished.[44] He also points out that a mistranslation of St. Jerome's version of the Bible, the Vulgate, is a third reason. Jerome translated Leviticus 19:26 to equate dreams with witchcraft, so that the text reads: "You shall not practice augury nor observe dreams" instead of the more acceptable translation: "Do not practice divination or soothsaying."[45] This mistranslation had a strongly negative influence on the Christian evaluation of dreams since the Vulgate was authoritative during the Middle Ages.

Kelsey wishes to return to the earlier attitude when dreams were considered the principle way God speaks to human beings. He feels that pastors and lay people should be aware of this important spiritual path. Attention to dreams can provide pastors with a way to understand the spiritual and psychological state of people with whom they work. Kelsey argues that since dreams reveal the personality's innermost condition, they inevitably deal with a person's relationship to God. Pastors could help people understand the symbolic language of dreams since this is the same symbolic language that the Church has always used to speak about the world of God and the spirits.

Kelsey believes that people can understand their own dreams without professional help. While some understand their dreams better than others, everyone can develop some skill in dream interpretation if they work at it. Kelsey suggests that we write down our dreams in order to have a complete record of dreams, fragments as well as longer dreams. Such a dream journal records a person's encounter with spiritual reality. Interpreting dreams becomes easier as we become familiar with the symbolic language that dreams speak. Kelsey suggests that we find another person to talk with about our dream experiences. A trained analyst or minister is not essential for this work but rather anyone who is interested in spiritual matters and open to the possibility of meaning in dreams could help us understand our dreams.

Kelsey follows Jung when he says that dream figures usually refer to aspects of our own personalities. He also adds that in a spiritual interpretation of dreams we must at least consider the hypothesis that a non-physical reality may interact with humans in dreams.[46] Even if we interpret dreams primarily as reflections of our personalities, they may still communicate a message or perspective from the spiritual realm. For Kelsey, taking dreams seriously from the religious point of view can reveal a new realm of religious experience.

Robert Johnson is another Jungian writer who has presented a straight-forward method for people to interpret dreams on their own. He identifies these four essential steps in understanding dreams: 1) find associations for each dream element; 2) connect dream images to specific characteristics in yourself; 3) interpret the dream by combining the associations in step one with the dynamics of your mental life shown in step two; 4) carry out rituals to make the dream concrete.[47] Johnson believes that people can work productively on their own psychological life but he advises them to have someone to call upon if they lose their bearings.

For Johnson the goal of inner work is to bring about a dialogue between the interior parts of ourselves so that fragmented pieces of the person may be fashioned into a unity. Dreams provide a starting point for inner work since they furnish a symbolic portrait of how various aspects of our personalities interact within us. Johnson suggests that we think of these personality parts as actual persons living inside us because that allows us to explore our inner life more fully.

When struggling with alternative interpretations of a dream or dream figure, Johnson says we should write out the contrasting interpretations to see which one illuminates the dream more fully. Some interpretations simply wither away in the process of writing them out. He also gives these general hints on how to decide upon a valid interpretation: 1) Choose the interpretation that shows you something you didn't know; 2) avoid the interpretation that inflates your ego or is self congratulatory and 3) avoid the interpretation that shifts responsibility away from yourself.[48]

One of the most interesting features of Johnson's approach is his insistence on rituals involving dream figures and plots. By ritual he means any act in honor of your dream. According to Johnson the best rituals are physical acts, solitary and silent.[49] The ritual may have something specifically to do with a dream, such as painting a dream symbol, but it may be unconnected to the dream plot, such as lighting a candle or walking around the block. Whatever the ritual, it registers at the deepest level of the psyche, and this maintains rapport between the conscious and the unconscious.

Another work that contributes to democratizing dream interpretation is Patricia Garfield's *Creative Dreaming*. She considers how other cultures have dealt with their dreams and gleans techniques and principles of dream appreciation from them. She believes that ordinary dreamers can understand their own dreams and also learn to work creatively with them.

In the Senoi tribe Garfield discovers techniques for controlling dreams.[50] The Senoi teach their children to establish friendly relationships with dream characters and to confront threatening dream figures. This procedure requires a certain degree of self-consciousness during the dream. In order to develop this ability Garfield suggests that while awake we should carry on an imaginary conversation with the characters that have already appeared in past dreams. By posing questions to these previous dream images before or after sleep we can eventually learn to relate to and question these characters during a dream.

This is actually a form of lucid dreaming which means that we become conscious of dreaming while in the dream. Lucid dreaming enables us to confront dream characters as the dream is happening. Further aspects of lucid dreaming deal with various transformations while dreaming (e.g. flying, becoming invisible, leaving the body, etc.) as well as with modifying the plot of a dream as it unfolds.

Garfield tends to overemphasize the manipulative role of consciousness in setting up dream experiences. She speaks of inducing a desired dream by formulating the type of dream sought (e.g. "Tonight I shall fly in my dream") and then concentrating on the images we wish to dream about. Such "dream incubation" seems to work with some dreamers but how much conscious control can or should be exercised in dreams? If dreams can be consciously controlled, to what extent can dream images be considered potentially objective manifestations of the psyche, or of the divine or spirit world? Of course, the fact that some dreams can be manipulated by conscious control before or during the dream does not automatically exclude the more objective character of other dreams.[51]

Gayle Delaney's *Living Your Dreams* explores the phenomenon of dream incubation and its usefulness for ordinary dreamers. Like Garfield, she describes an effective method of dream incubation that can be used by most people.[52] Her orientation is primarily problem-solving. She incubates a dream around a particular problem so that the dream will provide a solution that comes from the wisdom of the unconscious mind.

Here is her incubation method. First she discusses thoroughly the issue she wishes to dream about. The discussion should include the causes of the problem, various solutions that are presently recognized, and imagining what life would be like if the problem were solved. At the heart of her method is formulating an "incubation phrase" that compresses into one line a question or request clearly expressing the problem to be solved. An example of such a phrase might be "Help me to understand why I'm afraid of the dark." This phrase is then repeated over and over just before going to sleep.

Delaney states that the dreamer is responsible for each detail of the dream; this means that dream images do not refer to objective facts beyond the dreamer's own mind. In chapter four we shall see reasons for modifying such a statement. Yet so long as dreaming is not overly manipulated by conscious attempts to influence dream content dream incubation can be a valuable adjunct to dream interpretation. Even if consciousness is partially responsible for what we dream about (i.e. the general subject matter of our dreams) the incubated dream may still reveal aspects of external reality; God or the spirits might be present in a dream as an answer to an incubated question. For example, a person incubates a dream about choosing a vocation and then dreams that Jesus appears and calls her to the ministry. We might suppose that the dream symbol of Jesus is merely an aspect of the dreamer's mind attempting to solve her vocational dilemma. On the other hand, the dream symbol may actually evoke the presence of Jesus as a spiritual reality.

All the works mentioned here show an increasing recognition that dreams may have a wide variety of roles. Dream interpretation was greatly restricted when it was first introduced into psychology. In recent years, however, many of those who were initially interested in the psychological role of dreams have contributed to broadening the horizons of dream interpretation beyond those regions described by psychological theories.

This most recent development in dream interpretation shows a movement toward multiple interpretative hypotheses, i.e. realizing that dreams are not merely psychological portraits of the dreamer but may refer to various aspects of life. As dream interpretation develops within psychology and also moves beyond strictly psychological concerns we begin to see many dimensions of dreams that were neglected or consciously excluded in early psychological dream theories.

Faraday shows that dreams may be giving us valuable information about the external world. Faraday, Williams, Johnson, Ullman and Zimmerman show that dreams can lead to greater self-understanding and aid in solving all kinds of problems. Delaney shows how the problem-solving capacity of dreams can be consciously directed in dream incubation. Ullman and others have explored the psychic (especially the telepathic) potential of dreams. McLeester calls attention to the social and spiritual aspects of dreams. Williams, Sanford and

Kelsey emphasize the role of dreams as a spiritual path. Jones examines artistic inspiration in dreams. Garfield, Faraday and Williams explore the creative possibilities of working with dreams even to the point of becoming conscious while in the dream state and voluntarily creating dream adventures.

From an historical viewpoint we see that dream interpretation has gone through significant phases. Originally it was tied to a religious interpretation of dreams and was carried out in an authoritative mode. When dream interpretation was absorbed into psychology with the work of Freud the authoritative mode continued. Now, however, the authority did not work within a religious context but rather within the framework of a particular psychological theory. In both cases the dreamer was dependent on the interpretations of another person.

In all the books just cited we see a move from this authoritative mode to the mode of dream interpreter as facilitator rather than as the final authority on the meaning of dreams. With this development dreamers become more active participants in the process of discovering the meaning of their dreams and ultimately they are the final authority on the meaning of their own dreams. Dream interpretation is also recovering its earlier openness to the spiritual, psychic, creative and problem-solving dimensions of dreams. In this trend dream interpretation is moving beyond some of the restrictions imposed on it by various psychological theories.

But psychology has not had only a restrictive influence on dream interpretation. Dream interpretation has also benefited greatly from its engagement with psychology. Above all psychology has contributed scientific methodology to the ancient techniques of dream interpretation. Now we shall look at the broad movements in psychology to determine how they have contributed to methods in the present art and science of dream interpretation.

Notes

1. When I use the terms "God," "the gods," "religion" or "the divine" I do not necessarily refer to Judaism, Christianity and the God of Abraham, Isaac and Jacob. These terms may include the God described in the Judaic and Christian traditions, but they also extend beyond these traditions. The "divine" also includes various conceptions of ultimate reality or ultimate concern expressed in philosophical systems, non-theistic religions such as Taoism or Zen Buddhism and in the lives of ordinary people.
2. R. Van de Castle, "The Psychology of Dreaming," in *Dreams and Dreaming*, eds. S. Lee and A. Mayes (Middlesex, England, 1973), p. 17.
3. N. MacKenzie, *Dreams and Dreaming* (New York, 1965), pp. 29-30.
4. Later in this chapter we shall see that there is a renewed interest in the ancient practice of dream incubation.
5. Van de Castle, "Psychology of Dreaming," p. 19.
6. M. Kelsey, *God, Dreams and Revelation* (Minneapolis, 1974), pp. 17-122.
7. For example, Joseph was warned in a dream to flee to Egypt (Mt. 2:13) and to return from Egypt (Mt. 2:19-20).
8. Van de Castle, "Psychology of Dreaming," p. 18.
9. *Ibid.*, pp. 18-19.
10. C. Meier, *Die Bedeutung des Traumes* (Freiburg im Breisgau, 1972), pp. 71-74. Also see J. Sharma and L. Siegel, *Dream Symbolism in the Sramanic Tradition* (Calcutta, 1980), p. 41.
11. From Brihadarmyaka-Upanishad cited in *The New World of Dreams*, eds. R. Woods and H. Greenhouse (New York, 1974), p. 125.
12. W. O'Flaherty, *Dreams, Illusions and Other Realities* (Chicago, 1986), pp. 15-17.
13. E. von Grunebaum, "The Cultural Function of the Dream as Illustrated by Classical Islam," in *The Dream and Human Societies*, ed. E. von Grunebaum (Berkeley, 1962), p. 11.
14. R. Autra, *L'Interprétation des rêves dans la tradition Africaine* (Paris, 1983), p. 11.
15. R. S. Rattray, "Sex Dreams of the African Ashantis," in *The New World of Dreams*, p. 117.
16. D. Eggan, "Hopi Dreams in Cultural Perspective," in *Dream and Human Societies*, pp. 238 and 249.
17. A.I. Hallowell, "The Role of Dreams in Ojibwa Culture," in *Dream and Human Societies*, p. 282.
18. G. Devereux, "Pathogenic Dreams in Non-Western Societies," in *Dream and Human Societies*, p. 222.
19. C. Meier, "The Dream in Ancient Greece and Its Use in Temple Cures," in *Dream and Human Societies*, p. 305.
20. E. Fromm, *The Forgotten Language* (New York, 1957), p. 126.

21. Kelsey, *God, Dreams and Revelation*, pp. 165-166.
22. W. Wolff, *The Dream: Mirror of Conscience* (Westport, Conn., 1952), pp. 27-29.
23. A. Beguin, *L'âme romantique et le rêve* (Paris, 1939), pp. 45 and 99.
24. *Ibid.*, pp. 233-36.
25. *Ibid.*, pp. 299-302.
26. *Ibid.*, pp. 361-62.
27. B. Knapp, *Dream and Image* (New York, 1977), pp. 100-120.
28. *Ibid.*, pp. 330 and 357.
29. H. Ellenberger, *The Discovery of the Unconscious* (New York, 1970), pp. 303-304.
30. See the section on transpersonal psychology in chapter two for a discussion of Jung's viewpoints on religious phenomena in dreams.
31. See Erich Fromm's *The Forgotten Language* and Erik Erikson's "The Dream Specimen in Psychoanalysis," *Journal of the American Psychoanalytic Association*, 2 (1954), 5-56.
32. A. Faraday, *The Dream Game* (New York, 1974), p. 69.
33. M. Ullman and N. Zimmerman, *Working With Dreams* (New York, 1979), p. 115.
34. *Ibid.*, p. 124.
35. *Ibid.*, p. 77.
36. S. Williams, *Jungian-Senoi Dreamwork Manual* (Berkeley, 1980), p. 20.
37. Contamination here means that the analyst's ideas, attitudes and feelings are unconsciously imposed on a dream and then "discovered" in the dream so that the dreamer learns about the analyst's view but not necessarily what the dream is saying.
38. These Jungian and Gestalt techniques for working with dreams will be described in chapter two.
39. D. McLeester, *Welcome to the Magic Theater* (Amherst, Mass., 1977), p. 16.
40. *Ibid.*, pp. 21-24.
41. R. Jones, *The Dream Poet* (Cambridge, Mass., 1979), p. 28.
42. *Ibid.*, p. 117.
43. J. Sanford, *Dreams, God's Forgotten Language* (Philadelphia, 1968), p. 41.
44. On page 20 of this chapter.
45. I have quoted the Confraternity-Douay version here. Jerome also mistranslated Deuteronomy 18:10 in the same way.
46. Kelsey, *God, Dreams and Revelation*, p. 225.
47. R. Johnson, *Inner Work* (New York, 1986), pp. 45-55.
48. *Ibid.*, pp. 94-95.
49. *Ibid.*, p. 99.
50. P. Garfield, *Creative Dreaming* (New York, 1974), pp. 80-117.
51. "Objective" in this context means that the dream symbols reflect realities apart from the conscious manipulation of the dreamer's mind.
52. G. Delaney, *Living Your Dreams* (New York, 1979), pp. 21-26.

Chapter II

Dream Interpretation in Psychology

Experimental Psychology

In psychology there are four general approaches to the study of the psyche. Abraham Maslow, Anthony Sutich, Roberto Assagioli and others have called these approaches the four forces of psychology, referring to 1) experimental psychology and/or behaviorism, 2) psychoanalysis, 3) humanistic psychology and 4) transpersonal psychology.[1]

Experimental psychology has its roots back in the middle of the 19th century with the research of Wilhelm Wundt and Gustav Fechner in Leipzig (now in East Germany). Their work represented the first attempts to establish laboratory methods that would take psychological thought out of its previous *philosophical* context of reflection. They wanted to establish psychology as an empirical science akin to the natural sciences, based solidly on experiments that produce clear and measurable data. At Harvard University William James followed this trend by forming one of the first psychology laboratories in North America.

The factors that can be included in the design of an experimental study are limited to those which are measurable and quantifiable. Here the ingenuity of the experimental design is crucial because it determines the degree to which experimental psychology can include important areas of human experience. Professor Charles Tart, both an experimental and humanistic psychologist, describes this methodological problem: "Undergraduates begin to major in psychology and find that we concentrate our research efforts of methodologically sophisticated approaches on what seem to them trivial problems."[2] Tart regrets that experimental psychology has traditionally treated many vital areas of psychological interest such as religious experience, hypnosis, meditation and mysticism as relics of less enlightened times rather than phenomena to be seriously examined and understood.[3]

The experimental method tends to see questions of conscience, values, good and evil as metaphysics and therefore outside the problems of psychology. Faced with this model of psychology as one of the natural sciences, even Freud's psychoanalysis was not considered "hard science." In Freud's *New Introductory Lectures on Psychoanalysis* he complained about this limitation of science to "experimental methods":

"Only quite a short while ago the medical faculty in an American University refused to allow psycho-analysis the status of a science on the ground that it did not admit of any experimental proof. They might have raised the same objection to astronomy; indeed, experimentation with the heavenly bodies is particularly difficult. There one has to fall back on observation."[4]

Freud insisted that there are a variety of scientific methods and experimental psychology is but one approach to the study of the psyche. Most clinical approaches to psychology follow Freud's view that the observation of human thought, emotions and behavior takes the place of laboratory experiments. This feature does not make the clinical methods less empirical or less scientific than laboratory methods; it merely highlights the fact that each scientific method has its strengths and weaknesses. The strength of the experimental method is its capacity to quantify and compare psychological phenomena; its weakness is its inability to deal adequately with profound levels of psychological and spiritual experience.

Experimental psychology has influenced our understanding of dreams primarily through laboratory studies of the physiology of dreaming. Since 1953, with the work of N. Kleitman and E. Aserinsky at the University of Chicago, laboratory studies have contributed greatly to our understanding of sleep, patterns of brain activity in the various stages of sleep, and the physiological changes that occur during dreaming. Such studies indicate that there is a general rhythm to the sleep cycle which recurs during the night in segments that average from 70 to 90 minutes. The first REM dream period[5] occurs approximately 90 minutes after falling asleep and is only 5 to 10 minutes long; but the dream periods get progressively longer throughout the night and the last one may be more than 45 minutes. Since we are more likely to remember dreams if we wake up during a dream, this last long dream period of the night is the usual occasion for remembering and recording dreams.

There is also some dreamlike activity that occurs outside of the REM periods (termed non-REM or NREM dreams), but these dreams are usually more like waking thoughts. They are also less vivid and less dramatic than the dreams that occur during an REM period. All attempts to monitor dream activity show that dreaming is part of a natural biological process that occurs in everyone. The physiological changes that characterize REM periods are rapid eye movements (REM's), increased and irregular respiration, heart beat and blood pressure, paralysis of the large muscles, twitching of the small muscles, partial or full erection in males, and vaginal lubrication in females.[6]

There have also been some intriguing experimental studies in regard to the incorporation of somatic and external stimuli in dreams, the hypnotic investigation of dreams, dream recall, dream deprivation, the effects of drugs on dreaming, sleepwalking, sleeptalking, enuresis, lucid dreaming and the analysis of dream content.[7] It is beyond the scope of this book to discuss these experimental studies but there is one development here that is relevant to our examination of dream interpretation, namely the content analysis of dreams. In the dream content studies experimental psychology has gone beyond its concern with the physiological process of dreaming to get at the *meaning* of dreams. Measurement and quantification of data as well as the use of a control group, important features of experimental psychology, are involved in the content analysis of dreams.

Content analysis is a general method that extends well beyond dream interpretation and was developed to provide a quantitative analysis of verbal material. A dream report is merely one type of verbal material that makes use of this analytical method. Content analysis breaks down verbal material into its basic constituent elements. In dream interpretation these elements are counted and classified according to a standard list of categories, some of which we shall see shortly. The frequency of occurrence of various elements in these categories can then be used as a basis for comparing one person's dreams with another person's dreams or with normative frequencies for certain categories drawn from the averages of thousands of dreams.[8]

For example, a researcher may wish to study the significance of animals (or a specific animal, such as a dog or cat) in a person's dreams. In content analysis you would count all the instances of animals in a series of that person's dreams and compare this number with the normal frequency established for that person's culture, age and sex. A large deviation from the norm would indicate an unusual preoccupation with animals or with a particular animal although it would not necessarily indicate the psychological meaning of that preoccupation.[9]

Here is a chart summarizing the principal steps in the content analysis of dreams:

Content Analysis of Dreams

1. Interpret the dream as a picture: what do you see in each image or sequence.
2. Decompose the dream into a set of elements.
3. Classify elements using a standard list of categories.
4. Determine the frequency of each category.
5. Compare frequencies with those of a normative or comparison group.

Research objectives determine the categories that are used to analyze a person's dreams. A researcher may formulate categories where something unusual appears in dream reports. For example, a dreamer may appear to have a great number of friendly interactions or a preponderance of female figures in a series of dreams. The categories "friendly interactions" or "female dream characters" would then serve to objectify and quantify the researcher's impressions. The frequency of these categories would be compared with standard frequencies for these categories to determine if this is an unusual preoccupation. As noted above such a procedure does not determine the psychological meaning of this preoccupation, but it does help to locate and objectify possible problem areas in a personality.

Categories may also be derived from various personality theories. For instance, if you wish to study the super-ego in a person's dreams, you would note every instance where Freud points to a super-ego figure in his dream studies. Then count all the occasions where the person's dream reports fit Freud's descriptions of the super-ego. The number of times the super-ego appears in this person's dreams can then be compared with super-ego frequency in a control or comparison group. The content analyst must be thoroughly conversant with a particular personality theory in order to derive categories that accurately reflect that theory.

Calvin Hall, formerly professor of psychology at the University of California, Santa Cruz, has been the major researcher in dream-content analysis for over thirty years. His early work, *The Meaning of Dreams*, remains a classic in the field. The overall goal of dream-content analysis is to predict behavior, attitudes and feelings of a person from the frequency of certain dream contents. Unlike other methods of dream interpretation that we shall consider, this method requires a long series of dreams for effective analysis. Usually a series of 100 dreams is necessary to give an accurate and comprehensive picture of the dreamer's personality.

Hall's approach also differs from the more clinical methods of dream interpretation in that he has sampled dreams from the population at large rather than the more limited sampling of patients in psychotherapy or psychoanalysis. His conclusions regarding characteristic dream themes are based on the dreams of thousands of relatively "normal" people.

There are a number of typical categories Hall looks for as he analyzes dream reports: First he notes the setting of the dream. Does the dream occur indoors or outdoors? Is the setting familiar or unfamiliar? Is it realistic or distorted? There are many other ways in which settings could be classified as well, such as what room of the house does the dream take place in, or whether the dream reflects urban or rural life. On the basis of thousands of dream reports from men and women in various cultures Hall has been able to determine typical frequencies regarding many of these categories of dream life. For example in regard to dream settings, Hall found that women dream of being in familiar indoor settings more often than men do and that more dreams take place in familiar settings than unfamiliar ones for both men and women.[10] Such observations as these have led Hall to the conclusion that dreams reflect the waking life preferences and activities of the dreamer.[11]

Another typical category that Hall notes is objects that appear in dreams. Some of the most frequent objects in dreams are buildings, automobiles, trees, hats, coats and tools. For Hall the frequency of the objects indicates the dreamer's preferences and preoccupations. Dream characters represent another important category. Hall's records show that the people we dream about most frequently are the ones we are closest to in waking life: husbands and wives dream about each other; parents and children dream about each other. Still other typical categories for analyzing dreams are body parts, prominent persons, animals, interactions between dream characters, success and failure in dreams, good fortune and misfortune in dreams, and the emotions experienced in dreams.

Hall sees content analysis as particularly valuable in examining a large number of dreams. The variety and number of characters, objects, settings, interactions and emotions in a long series of dreams is very difficult to understand without resorting to a system of classification that can quantify these categories and relate them to personality trends.

Simply noting the frequency of a theme indicates that it is a preoccupation of the dreamer. According to Hall, if you dream frequently about failing in dreams, you are preoccupied with failure. Hall studies the frequency of a dream element or theme by comparing it with the norm established for that category. The norms are the average frequencies obtained from the analysis of many dream series of "normal" people. Regarding the category of failure in dreams, for example, norms show that young American males dream of failing in 13 of every 100 dreams. If you have 30 failure dreams out of a series of 100 you would be unusually preoccupied with failure in your life.

As an illustration of the content-analytical method and its potential applications, we shall consider Hall's analysis of the dreams of Freud and Jung. In 1968 he applied a content analysis to the published dreams of the two pioneers of modern dream interpretation.[12] This example shows the value of a quantitative analysis of dreams for a comparative portrait of two important historical figures.[13]

From Freud he considered 28 dreams from *The Interpretation of Dreams* and *On Dreams* and from Jung he examined 31 dreams appearing in *Memories, Dreams, Reflections*. Here are some of the observations Hall was able to make on the basis of his content analysis of their dreams. I shall present these observations in two parts: part one will be the data generated from the content analysis and part two will be Hall's interpretation of the data. Hall himself reminds us that content analysis only generates data, it does not interpret. To make sense out of the data and determine its psychological significance remains largely the subjective task of the investigator.

Data: Jung's dreams were filled with scenery, architecture and objects rather than people.

Interpretation: Jung was more solitary than Freud, and would keep disciples more at a distance.

Data: There were more animals in Jung's dreams than in Freud's.

Interpretation: Jung identifies more closely than Freud with the world of nature.

Data: There were more mystical, fictional and historical

figures in Jung's dreams.

Interpretation: Jung lived more in the past, Freud more in the present.

Data: Jung's dreams were more about members of his family. Freud's dreams were more about friends and acquaintances.

Interpretation: Jung's sociability was expressed more in the immediate family; Freud's social life was more outside the family.

Data: Jung usually initiates the friendly encounters in dreams while Freud receives the friendliness.

Interpretation: Freud wanted people to respond to him in a friendly manner while Jung had more social autonomy.

Data: Re. aggressive interactions in the dreams: Jung showed the same pattern as the average male dream: more aggressive interactions with men than women. Freud showed the reverse of the typical pattern; he had more aggression with females than males and many more friendly encounters with men than women.

Interpretation: According to the normal Oedipus complex, we would expect a man to be more hostile to men and friendly to women. Jung's dreams conformed to the normal Oedipus complex while Freud's dreams typified an inverted Oedipus complex that is associated with emotional homosexuality. Hall notes that Freud spoke of overcoming his emotional homosexuality.

Data: Jung had an equal amount of success and failure in dreams. Freud had much more success than failure in his dreams.

Interpretation: According to the norms for male dreamers, men have an equal amount of success and failure in dreams. Jung is average here while Freud is untypical in this category. Freud was more preoccupied with success and more strongly motivated to succeed than was Jung.

Data: Freud had no good fortune in his dreams while Jung had more good fortune than the average male dreamer.[14]

Interpretation: Freud saw his success as a result of his own efforts while Jung was more fatalistic, seeing his success due to forces outside his power.

These are some of the observations Hall makes in his analysis. Hall's interpretation of the data squares with what we know about both Freud and Jung from biographical accounts. He sees this as evidence supporting the continuity theory of dreams, i.e. that dreams furnish a symbolic portrait of the dreamer that is like (continuous with) the dreamer's waking life.[15]

This article is a good example of the creative possibilities for applying content analysis to dreams. The content analysis of dreams has contributed a quantitative and comparative assessment to dream interpretation. Unfortunately Hall's content analysis is technical and not easily applied by ordinary dreamers. To this extent the experimental approach has not noticeably advanced the movement toward democratizing dream interpretation. Yet Hall's analysis of dreams has helped ordinary people to understand their own dreams. He insists that the dream is a picture language that portrays the dreamer's preoccupations and everyone can interpret a picture.[16] This viewpoint gives people the confidence they need to approach their own dreams. In Hall's view even if the dreamer only notices the setting of the dream this sheds light on the dreamer's world-view and basic attitude toward life.

Content analysis has also established certain norms for what ordinary people dream about. Since the advent of psychoanalysis, psychology has explored the role of dreams primarily in neurotic and psychotic patients. Hall helped to shift this focus of dream study from abnormal to normal psychology. His studies have determined what kinds of actions, objects, persons and settings occur in the dreams of ordinary people. While content analysis holds that dreams should be interpreted as pictures, it does not suggest a method of association by which the dream picture may be connected to the dreamer's life. For such qualitative methods of dream interpretation we look to the other forces of psychology.

Notes

1. A. Sutich, "Statement of Purpose," *Journal of Transpersonal Psychology*, 1/1 (1969), p. i.
2. C. Tart, *Altered States of Consciousness* (Garden City, N. J., 1972), p. 4.
3. There has been some development of experimental psychology to include these more interesting areas of psychological research as can be seen in the volume Tart edited: *Altered States of Consciousness.*
4. *New Introductory Lectures on Psychoanalysis, SE*, XXII, p. 22.
5. REM refers to the "rapid eye-movements" that accompany the dream state.
6. Milton Kramer (ed.), *Dream Psychology and the New Biology of Dreaming* (Springfield, Illinois, 1969), pp. 5-37.
7. Here I shall cite only a few volumes where these studies are presented and/or reviewed: *Experimental Studies of Dreaming* (eds. H. Watkin and H. Lewis) presents and reviews recent experimental approaches to dream recall, dream deprivation, sleepwalking, sleeptalking, enuresis, and the effects of drugs on dreaming. The list of references at the end of that work will also guide the reader to other studies in the laboratory investigation of dreams. *Dreams and Dreaming* (eds. A. Mayes and S. Lee) contains a number of experimental studies and bibliographical details on many other laboratory studies. Wm. Domhoff reviews the experimental studies on dream control and the incorporation of desired psychological traits in dreams (*The Mystique of Dreams*, pp. 88-94). Also see E. Hartmann's *The Biology of Dreaming* and I. Oswald's *Sleeping and Waking* for more information on the physiological study of dreaming.
8. C. Hall and R. Lind, *Dreams, Life and Literature: A Study of Franz Kafka* (Chapel Hill, North Carolina, 1970), p. 12.
9. *Ibid.,* p. 12.
10. Calvin Hall, *The Meaning of Dreams*, pp. 21-46.
11. *Ibid.*, pp. 71-89.
12. C. Hall and W. Domhoff, "The Dreams of Freud and Jung," *Psychology Today*, 2/1 (June, 1968), 42-45; 64-65.
13. Hall and Richard Lind also carried out an extensive content analysis of Franz Kafka's dreams to demonstrate how this quantitative method can shed light on the inner life of a major literary figure. See *Dreams, Life and Literature.*
14. The category "good fortune" is defined as something good happening in the dream through no effort on the dreamer's part and through no friendly intent on another character's part.
15. The continuity theory is often contrasted with the compensation theory of dreams, according to which dreams compensate for our waking life experience and thus provide a picture that looks very different from the dreamer's conscious perspective and waking life.

16. "They (dreams) are pictures of what the mind is thinking. Anyone who can look at a picture and say what it means ought to be able to look at his dream pictures and say what they mean . . . Any clear-headed person should be able to interpret dreams." *The Meaning of Dreams*, p. 85.

Freud's Interpretation: Psychoanalysis

Freud introduced many of the basic principles presupposed in contemporary methods of understanding dreams. The day's residue in dreams, association to each of the dream images, the various stimuli that influence dreams and the dream-work mechanisms are basic elements in Freud's interpretation of dreams.

A striking characteristic of Freud's method of dream analysis is that the dream as it is remembered (the manifest dream) is not the most important part of the dream. The dream characters and actions that we see on the dream stage are for Freud merely the starting point for discovering what thoughts, feelings and events inspired a particular dream. These underlying elements represent the latent dream and for Freud this is the essence of the dream.

He maintains that these essential dream thoughts are converted into the manifest dream images, feelings and actions by means of certain dream-work mechanisms. For Freud these mechanisms help to disguise the latent dream thoughts. Since he considers dreams to be the hidden fulfillment of repressed wishes Freud supposes that unconsciously the dreamer censors the forbidden wishes by distorting these wishes through the dream-work mechanisms. He describes a number of these mechanisms that convert the latent dream: condensation, displacement and dramatic representation are the principal ones.

Condensation refers to Freud's observation that the original dream thoughts are much longer than the dream as remembered. Where the manifest dream may be only half a page long, the underlying dream-thoughts may require a dozen times as much space. In condensation the manifest dream omits some elements from the latent dream and compresses (or condenses) other elements into a single new image.[1] For instance, two people, feelings or memories might be joined into a single image as when in the manifest dream you see a teacher who at the same time looks like your father. This is a dramatic way of showing how certain people or memories are connected in the dreaming mind.

Displacement indicates that feelings, attitudes, or meanings attached to an element in the latent dream change as the element enters the manifest dream. An element of greater importance or emotional intensity in the latent dream may appear unimportant in the manifest dream or a peripheral aspect of the latent dream appears in the manifest dream as central and charged with great emotion.[2] Displacing the emotional charge or the importance of a latent dream element distorts and disguises the underlying dream wishes and is, for Freud, an expression of dream censorship. The ego resists seeing the latent dream wishes in the original form. Freud gives this example of displacement from one of his own dreams: "I saw before me his face (Freud's friend) . . . A yellow beard that surrounded it stood out especially clearly." Freud explains that the beard which formed the center-point of the manifest dream had no connection with the meaning of the latent dream which dealt with his own ambitious wishes. So here an insignificant point in the latent dream was displaced to give it center stage in the manifest dream.

The third main dream-work mechanism is dramatic representation. This consists in transforming thoughts into visual images and representing feelings, attitudes, and other inner experiences as if they were sensory experiences happening in the outer world.[3] This dream-work process is the foundation of the subjective interpretation of dreams. From the perspective of dramatic representation elements in the dream are aspects of the dreamer's personality. We shall see in the next section how influential this assumption has been in humanistic psychology and it has been a basic assumption in clinical dream interpretation within each of the general forces of psychology.

Attention to this dream-work mechanism is partially responsible for the psychoanalytic tendency to interpret so many symbols of external objects as sexual symbols. Such symbols are thought to reflect the dreamer's attitude toward various aspects of sexuality. This consistently brings the interpretation around to the feelings and attitudes of the subject (the dreamer) and away from understanding these symbols as representing objective realities and situations in the external world. For instance, in his *Introductory Lectures on Psychoanalysis*, Freud interprets many dream symbols in this way.[4] Reptiles, fish, snakes, hats, overcoats, water-taps, fountains, hanging lamps, pencils, pen-holders, nail-files, hammers, balloons, airplanes, sticks, umbrellas, trees, knives, spears, rifles, pistols—all represent the male organ. The female genitals (including breasts and pubic hair) may be represented by the following dream symbols: pits, cavities, vessels, bottles, boxes, trunks, cases, chests, pockets, cupboards, stoves, doors, gates, snails, mussels, the mouth, churches, chapels, apples, peaches, woods, bushes and jewel-cases. All these visual images could represent the dreamer's attitude and feelings about sex. Seeing dramatic representation as a primary dream-work mechanism, psychoanalytic dream interpretation emphasizes the subjective level of dream interpretation with a clearly sexual cast.

These are the principal dream-work mechanisms that Freud assumes transform the latent dream wishes into the manifest dream. For Freud dream analysis consists in reversing this dream-work. Therefore the first step in Freud's method is to have the patient state the manifest dream (using no notes) so that he can begin to work from the manifest dream back toward the latent dream thoughts through a process of association.

After presenting the dream the patient associates to each element of the manifest dream. The dreamer says whatever comes to mind in relation to each dream image or action. Because Freud does not consider the manifest dream to be central he advocates free association to the dream images. Thus the chain of association leads wherever it will regardless of how far these thoughts diverge from the manifest dream elements and action. For example, the dream image of a horse galloping out of control toward a lake might lead to various memories of horses that in turn might lead to the place where you first rode a horse, to the people you met then, to the time when you were seven years old, or to whatever else might come to mind. In such a line of association it is not necessary to return to the specific dream image and the particular action or context of that image in the dream.

Freud points out that his procedure of free association calls for a special attitude of attention that is not like reflection.[5] He underscores the more passive cast of mind necessary for free association. Reflection is excluded because it involves an active search of the conscious mind rather than simply allowing associations to emerge on their own from the unconscious mind without consciously censoring them.

The associated memories, feelings and thoughts expand from the dream images to form the psychological network that underlies the original manifest dream. This thought web created by free association helps to establish the reference of the manifest dream images, that is, it aids the analyst in discovering what aspect of the dreamer's life the dream is commenting upon.

Freud recognizes that there is a link between the dream images and "groups of strongly emotional thoughts and interests" that are the complexes.[6] For him the chain of free association is the link that leads from the manifest dream images to the complexes. Because dream images express underlying complexes, associations to these images will also be connected to the complexes since the same unconscious activity generates both the dream images and the associations to those dream images. The complexes are therefore the real constituent elements of the latent dream and are the "concealed unconscious material we are in search of."[7]

Freud also considers that all other dreams of the same night are a part of any particular dream interpretation. He calls these dreams of a single night homologous dreams and says they all comment on the same underlying instinctual impulse.[8] This marks the beginning of a recognition that dreams can be interpreted in a series and not simply as isolated specimens of psychological life. We have already seen that Calvin Hall's content analysis examines a whole series of dreams and we shall see that Carl Jung's method also considers the dream series. Dreams in a series offer various symbolic descriptions of a problem or situation and this provides a more comprehensive picture of the problem.

A further step in determining what latent dream thoughts are behind the manifest dream is to consider the events of the days immediately preceding the dream. Freud calls these impressions from a day or two before the dream the "day's residues." He says in every dream we can find a point of contact with experiences of the previous day, even though these recent impressions are frequently unnoticed by the waking memory.[9] Dreams may also draw upon material from other times in the dreamer's past so long as such memories are linked to experiences of the day before the dream.

Freud says that "regularly formed" dreams stand on two legs: 1) the current exciting cause (from the day's residue) and 2) some momentous event in childhood.[10] The dream connects the childhood event (or wish) with the event of the previous day. He sees the connection as an attempt "to reshape the present on the model of the remote past."[11] For Freud the day's residue (current event) is not sufficient in itself to inspire a dream, but will precipitate a dream only if it connects with a childhood wish in the unconscious.

To understand a person's dreams Freud also considers the present circumstances and life history of the dreamer. This provides the life context within which the dream symbols can be understood. In this way Freud determines whether the dream is referring primarily to the subjective state of the dreamer and/or to persons in the external world. Generally if a dream character is very much a part of the dreamer's life, someone the dreamer sees regularly, then the dream probably refers to that person. For instance, if a woman dreams of her sister who lives with her, the dream image of the sister probably refers to the actual person of the sister. This would be the objective level of reference. On the other hand, if the woman dreams of an old school mate she has not seen for thirty years, the dream image of the school mate probably refers to an aspect of the dreamer's own personality that is like the school mate. This would be the subjective level of reference.[12]

Determining the subjective or objective reference of the manifest dream images helps to indicate what the latent dream thoughts are about. The network of free associations to the dream images adds to the total picture of the dream. For Freud the latent dream thoughts are a fundamental part of the overall analytical process. The analyst uses the latent dream thoughts along with the patient's other communications in order to reconstruct the forgotten childhood experiences that underlie the person's neurosis.

In order to show concretely how Freud's method contributes to dream interpretation I shall consider briefly his analysis of a dream of Dora, an eighteen-year old hysteric he treated in 1900.[13] She presented this dream to Freud:

> A house was on fire. My father was standing beside my bed and woke me up. I dressed quickly. Mother wanted to stop and save her jewel-case; but Father said: "I refuse to let myself and my two children be burnt for the sake of your jewel-case." We hurried downstairs, and as soon as I was outside I woke up.[14]

I shall not go into each detail of Freud's interpretation but consider only the main points to illustrate his method. He begins by asking Dora to tell him anything that occurs to her in connection with each part of the dream. Dora comes up with the following associations to elements in the dream:

An emergency in the night: Dora recalls a dispute between her father and mother about locking the dining-room door that was the only entrance to her brother's bedroom. The father did not want the door locked in case the boy might have to leave his room in the night.

The fire: Her father recently mentioned that he was afraid of fire when the family arrived at a small wooden house without a lightning rod.

The father standing beside the bed: She recalls that at the place where she had the dream, Herr K., a friend of her father, was actually standing beside her when she awoke from a nap. Herr K. had previously made advances toward Dora on a walk in the woods.

Dressing quickly: She decided to lock her bedroom door while she dressed quickly because Herr K. had come into the room unannounced on a previous occasion.

The jewel-case: Herr K. had given her a jewel-case.

Freud puts these associations together in this way: Dora blames her father for placing her in the proximity of Herr K. Her jewel-case (female genitals) is in danger from Herr K. The dream turns this into the opposite so that it is her father who saves her from fire and danger rather than places her in jeopardy. In her dream her father is standing beside her bed as Herr K. had actually done. Freud concludes that Dora repressed the thought that she was ready to give herself to Herr K. and that she was afraid of yielding to this temptation.

In this dream Freud sees Dora's unconscious, infantile, love for her father as the underlying wish that provides the motive power for forming the dream. He summarizes his interpretation of the dream this way:

> . . . The intention (Dora carried with her into sleep) might have been consciously expressed in some such words as these: "I must fly from this house, for I see that my virginity is threatened here; I shall go away with my father, and I shall take precautions not to be surprised while I am dressing in the morning." These thoughts were clearly expressed in the dream; they formed part of a mental current which had achieved consciousness and a dominating position in waking life. Behind them can be discerned obscure traces of a train of thought which formed part of a contrary current and had consequently been suppressed. This train of thought culminated in the temptation to yield to the man . . .[15]

Freud's reasoning makes sense in the context of this case, up to the point of suggesting that Dora repressed her desire for Herr K. Rather, the dream expresses anxiety about the situation with Herr K. Three of the images in this short dream refer to Dora's present circumstances in regard to Herr K: 1) the dream image of her father standing next to her bed is like the startling occasion where Herr K. was standing there; 2) her dressing quickly in the dream is similar to her waking experience of dressing quickly so Herr K. might not see her undressed; and 3) the jewel-case in the dream reminded Dora of the one which Herr K. had given to her. Dora's associations tie all of these dream images to her experiences with Herr K., but the dream shows anxiety about Herr K., not affection for him.

When Freud sees a repressed wish to yield to Herr K. his reconstruction of the traumatic experience goes beyond the images given in the dream. Dora's associations indicate that she was worried (a fire in the house, the jewel case being in danger) about Herr K. (a father-like figure standing beside her bed just as Herr K. had actually done). The dream shows her escaping, indicating she does not wish to be in this situation.

The image of the father-figure standing beside Dora's bed is very ambiguous. In the dream this figure wakens her and saves her from the fire; this connects the image with her love for her father and her wish for protection. But Dora's associations to this image also connect with the time when Herr K. actually stood beside her bed; in this regard the man is not her protector but the cause of her anxiety, Herr K. This mixed image of her father and Herr K. does indicate that Dora's attitude towards Herr K. was connected with her feelings about her father, and this may be where Freud detects in Dora an underlying current of affection for Herr K. The confused image more likely points to the question in Dora's mind about why her father placed her in jeopardy with his friend, Herr K.[16]

Even from this short dream interpretation the steps of Freud's method are nonetheless clear. The primary step of following the dreamer's associations is illustrated in this interpretation. The day's residue regarding Herr K. (that he had been standing beside her bed) points to the reference of the dream, indicating what Dora's anxiety is about. Freud also takes into account the dreamer's present circumstances (Dora's relationship to Herr K.) in determining the meaning of the dream. From Dora's conscious situation Freud interprets the fire primarily on the subjective level (reflecting Dora's anxiety) and he interprets the man standing at her bed primarily on the objective level (referring both to her father and to the time when Herr K. was actually standing there). He interprets the jewel case on both the subjective and objective levels (referring to her anxiety about her possible sexual relationship with Herr K. and to the jewel case that Herr K. had actually given her). From these considerations Freud arrives at both the latent meaning of the dream and how the dream sheds light on Dora's symptoms. The basic steps of this dream interpretation might be summed up in the following chart:

Elements in Freudian Dream Analysis

1. State manifest dream using no notes.
2. Free-associate to each element of the manifest dream. Do not censor any associations.
3. Consider the dream series, i.e. homologous dreams of the same night.[17]
4. Consider the dreamer's conscious situation (life history) and the day's residues in the dream.
5. Determine the subjective or objective reference of the dream.
6. Discern latent dream structures (the meaning of the dream).
7. Formulate analytical constructions based on the latent dream, i.e. show how the dream sheds light on the dreamer's development and symptoms.

Many of these elements in Freudian dream analysis are applicable to our method of dream interpretation. But certain theoretical aspects of psychoanalysis limit its contribution to dream interpretation in the psychology of religion. Freud emphasizes the sexual and aggressive elements that appear in dreams to the point of ignoring religious dream symbols. Also, Freud's world-view rules out an explicitly religious interpretation of dreams and to that extent his approach is discontinuous with the ancient art of dream interpretation that worked out of a religious context.

Dream interpretation in this century has broadened the parameters of what Freud observed in dreams and has offered alternative accounts of the psychological dynamics that generate dream phenomena. Now we turn to humanistic psychology, a major psychological movement that has offered an alternative view of the psyche and has opened the way for a more democratic and participatory approach to dream interpretation.

Notes

1. *Introductory Lectures on Psychoanalysis, SE* XV, p. 171.
2. *Ibid.*, pp. 208-109.
3. *Ibid.*, p. 175.
4. *Ibid.*, pp. 154-157.
5. *Ibid.*, p. 106.
6. *Ibid.*, p. 109.
7. *Ibid.*, p. 114.
8. *The Interpretation of Dreams, SE.* IV, p. 334.
9. *Ibid.*, p. 165.
10. Freud uses this analogy to describe the relationship between these two aspects of dream formation: "A daytime thought may very well play the part of *entrepreneur* for a dream; but the *entrepreneur*, who, as people say, has the idea and the initiative to carry it out, can do nothing without capital; he needs a *capitalist who can afford the outlay, and the capitalist who provides the psychical outlay for the dream is invariably and indisputably, whatever may be the thoughts of the previous day, a wish from the unconscious.*" "A Case of Hysteria," *SE* VII, p. 87.
11. *Ibid.*, p. 71.
12. Even at the objective level, the dreamer may still be experiencing her own attitudes toward her sister, yet the dream image probably refers to the sister and not to an aspect of the dreamer's personality. In the dream of the former school mate, that image could also refer potentially to someone or some situation in the dreamer's environment who reminded her of the school mate or of that period of her past.
13. P. McCaffrey considers Freud's interpretation of Dora's dream an excellent demonstration of Freud's dream theory. In his book, *Freud and Dora: The Artful Dream*, he carefully studies Freud's method of dream analysis and points out some of the problems with Freud's interpretation of Dora's dreams. McCaffrey argues that Freud's analysis ignores the structure and coherence of the manifest dream. This generally agrees with my criticism of Freud's interpretation.
14. "A Case of Hysteria," *SE* VII, p. 64.
15. *Ibid.*, p. 85.
16. McCaffrey notes that Freud sees his own role represented in this dream as similar to Herr K., not as Dora's father (a more likely transference interpretation of this dream). See *Freud and Dora: The Artful Dream* (New Brunswick, N.J., 1984), pp. 44-45. Freud sees that this dream could also reflect Dora's mistrust of him as well as of Herr K. since it could express her underlying attitude which eventually moved her to discontinue the analysis with Freud.
17. In this illustrative case, however, Freud does not deal with other dreams of the same night.

Humanistic Psychology

Humanistic psychology, the Third Force in psychology, emphasizes the primary role of consciousness and human responsibility.[1] Humanistic psychology criticizes behaviorism for ruling out a consideration of conscious experience and it objects to the psychoanalytic emphasis on unconscious over conscious factors in personality functioning. The Third Force resists all deterministic explanations: against the behaviorists it asserts that our actions are not determined by conditioning and against the psychoanalysts it insists that childhood experiences do not determine our feelings, thoughts, attitudes and actions.

Humanistic psychology is considered by some to be unscientific for rejecting all deterministic models of human functioning. It considers that human concerns and behaviors cannot be adequately accounted for merely as functions of sexuality, aggression or conditioning. Humanistic psychology has sought a more appropriate philosophical basis than the 19th-century positivism that reduces phenomena to material causes.

Two representatives of the existentialist wing of humanistic psychology, Ludwig Binswanger and Medard Boss, have turned to Martin Heidegger for philosophical guidance in working out their psychology. In contrast to psychological determinism they emphasize that humans reflect on the meaning of their existence and shape their lives through freedom and responsibility. Dream interpretation in humanistic psychology reflects this philosophical approach. Dream symbols reflect human values, relationships, decision-making, feelings, thoughts and attitudes that are the essential factors determining healthy or neurotic behavior.

Humanistic psychologists generally interpret dreams on the subjective level. They look for the dreamer's meaning system, which includes his or her world view, values and style of decision-making. I shall focus on one of the most influential schools in humanistic dream interpretation, the school of Gestalt Therapy, to illustrate the principles of humanistic dream interpretation in psychology. The guiding spirit of Gestalt dream interpretation was Fritz Perls who developed a method of enacting each element of the dream as an expression of the dreamer's own personality.

Gestalt dream work concentrates on the present experience of dream images, feelings and attitudes. To re-experience dream feelings in the "here and now" the dreamer tells the dream in the present tense. This involves the dreamer again in the immediate experience of the dream and avoids "talking about" the dream as if it happened in the past or to another person. Where other approaches tend to interpret and classify the dream contents rather than reliving them, Gestalt avoids interpreting the dream story.[2] In this approach the dreamer re-enters the feelings of the dream experience and is brought directly into contact with areas of experience that are still preoccupying the dreamer (what Gestaltists call "unfinished business"). Here the dreamer confronts directly the existential meaning of the dream.

The dream itself is not the central focus in Gestalt work and can be preempted by other emerging concerns. For instance, if the therapist notices a peculiar or symptomatic phrase, gesture or voice tone as the person presents the dream, this may become the focus for the rest of the dream work. A case cited in *Gestalt Therapy Verbatim* illustrates this characteristic of Gestalt dream work[3]:

Max: I have a fragment of a dream, Fritz.

Fritz: Well let's start right away. Until you understand the meaning of what we are doing you will see this as a kind of technique. And a technique that is not understood becomes a gimmick. So right now we'll use, in your sense, a certain amount of gimmicks. Now the gimmick I'd like to use with you is to change *having* into *being*.[4] Instead of "I *have* a fragment of a dream" you say "I *am* a fragment of a dream."

M: I am a fragment of a dream.

F: Now stay with this sentence and assimilate it. Could it make sense to you that you are a fragment of a dream?

M: Well, I'm a fragment of a whole . . . Only part of me is here.

F: You feel your reality; you're not a dream.

M: I feel the chair, I feel heat, I feel the tenseness in my stomach and in my hands—

F: The tenseness. Here we've got a noun. Now *the*
tenseness is a noun. Now change the noun, the thing, into a
verb.

M: I am tense. My hands are tense.

F: Your hands are tense. They have nothing to do with you.

M: I am tense.

F: You are tense. How are you tense? . . .

This approach has the advantage of dealing with the most
immediate need expressed by the dreamer, or at least the central
gesture, phrase or voice tone that the Gestaltist notices, but it
frequently means that a dream does not receive complete or
thorough treatment. When Max finally gets around to telling
the dream, Fritz comments not directly on the dream but on the
gestures used in telling the dream:[5]

Fritz: What interested me mostly was you spoke about the
right side being maimed (in the dream) and yet all the time you
were only talking with your right hand. The left was completely
passive . . .

Max: My left hand is weak. I can do very little with it. My
right hand's a lot stronger . . .

Even when the work centers on elements of the dream itself
(rather than on the style of presentation or interruptions in the
free functioning of the organism[6]) this is frequently limited to a
few elements of the dream. The dreamer may enact a few of the
dream characters or dream elements in order to re-own the feelings, attitudes and insights connected with those aspects of the
dream.

This method is based on the view that each element of the
dream represents some aspect of the dreamer's personality and
the goal of dream work is to re-own all of these aspects of
psychological life that appear in the dream, many of which have
been excluded from awareness.[7] Thus dream work is designed to
broaden awareness and to re-own and express consciously feelings, attitudes and ideas that are unacceptable to the dreamer's
self-image and are consequently disowned. This procedure of
re-owning and enacting each of the dream elements is a major
step towards integration of psychological contents and for this

reason Perls speaks of dreams as the royal road to integration.[8]

Gestaltists frequently identify polar opposites in a dream such as in the following dream of Bob who just quit his secure job to return to school. He dreams of escaping from an attic window of a stately old house. He begins to climb on a rope ladder up a steep mountain face. He feels exhilarated about being on the mountain yet frightened of falling off the flimsy ladder. In this dream the desire for freedom (escaping from the attic and climbing the rope-ladder) is seen in sharp contrast to the need for security (the stately old house). Such opposites often represent basic conflicts within the personality.

The therapist usually asks the dreamer to bring the polar opposites into a dialogue by using the "hot seat" technique. The "hot seat" is merely an empty chair which is used to represent an aspect of the dreamer's personality. The dreamer can shuttle back and forth between chairs to establish a dialogue between two aspects of the personality, where each aspect is represented by the empty chair. This process has the advantage of externalizing various aspects of the personality so they may be dealt with in a concrete way. The emphasis here is on an experiential resolution of the conflict or at least a greater awareness of the various aspects of the conflict.

First the dreamer play-acts one aspect of the polarity. In the example of Bob's dream, Bob enacts his experience of exhilaration at being on the mountain ladder. Here Bob expresses the feelings, ideas and attitudes associated with the longing for freedom. Then he moves to the empty chair and expresses the feelings and ideas associated with the aspect of his personality which desires security. Here he enacts his experience of comfort and security in the stately old house. While shuttling back and forth between the two chairs and expressing in turn the attitudes represented by each chair some integration occurs between those two conflicting aspects of the personality.

Since Perls sees all elements of the dream as aspects of the dreamer's own personality, almost any two dream figures or images might be brought into dialogue in this fashion leading to a more integrated personality. Usually the therapist focuses on those elements of the dream that stand out as the dreamer tells the dream in the present tense. This approach places a large share of the responsibility for directing the dream work on the therapist, especially since the dreamer may only deal with one or two figures or symbols from a dream in a single Gestalt session.

The Gestalt method also emphasizes the value of expressing dreams and dream symbols in some artistic medium.[9] A Gestalt therapist often encourages the dreamer to draw, paint, sculpt, dance or sing dream images to heighten awareness of how the dream symbols represent disowned aspects of the personality. This kind of self-expression helps dreamers to become more aware of what they are feeling inside themselves. Judgments about the artistic quality of these exercises are irrelevant. The goal here is self-discovery, not creating art.

Elements in Gestalt Dream Work

1. State the dream text in the present tense.
2. Subjective hypothesis: All elements in the dream are parts of the dreamer's personality.
3. Dramatic enactment of dream images, feelings and plots.
4. Dramatic encounter and interaction of various dream elements.
5. Artistic expression of dream elements.

The Gestalt approach is an effective method for working on dreams with groups as well as with individuals. The advantage to group work is both economic and strategic. Clearly the cost of group therapy or dream work is more reasonable than the price of individual therapy. Also there is the additional value in group dream work of using the group for emotional support and for testing insights and behaviors gained in the dream work. In the protective setting of the group we can try out behavior that is portrayed in a dream.

There is also educational value in observing others doing dream work.[10] Since many of the themes expressed in dreams are common to the human situation, a group member often is able to identify with another's dream work and gain insights from observing how the dreamer deals with a dream. Frequently it is easier to understand the imagery in another's dream since we are not so defensive about that particular attitude, characteristic or feeling expressed in the other person's dream. Furthermore, when observing another's dream work, the dynamics of dreams become clearer. Again, it is often easier to notice how dreams symbolize certain personality characteristics or personal conflicts in another person since we do not have to guard against painful recognition or the responsibility to act upon the insights of the dream work.

A disadvantage of Gestalt group work is the tendency to focus on only certain elements of the dream. This is due, in part, to the time restriction since it is impractical to go through each element of a dream when there are a number of people waiting to work on their own dreams. This feature of group work, added to the Gestalt tendency to move away from the dream contents in favor of any other emergent need or interruption of organismic functioning, contributes to a partial rather than complete treatment of dreams.

A major strength of the Gestalt approach to dreams is that in the dramatic enactment of the dream symbols and figures, there is no predetermined interpretation imposed on the symbols. As the dreamer gets into the experience of enacting a dream character the impressions of the moment emerge spontaneously and may have a bearing on virtually any aspect of life. In this method of total involvement, direct experience and expression of the emotions associated with dream symbols overcome intellectual resistances and expectations of what the symbols could mean.

Precisely when the dreamer is caught up in the experience of enacting a dream character, she is more likely to slip into memories and associations that might not have occurred to her if she had been merely reflecting on possible meanings of that dream character or trying to remember experiences associated with that character. She may not even be aware of some of the things she is saying or their possible significance, so the Gestaltist heightens the dreamer's awareness by having her repeat significant phrases that just popped out of her mouth, or explore further the implications of some aspects of the dream enactment.

Gestalt therapy as represented by Fritz Perls tend to limit the interpretation of dream symbols to the subjective level, and humanistic psychology in general interprets psychological symbols as reflecting human potential.[11] From this viewpoint even the God symbol is seen to express and conserve the highest human values. Theoretically this would limit the interpretation of dream symbols so that religious symbols would be reduced to particular human values. This approach would seem to rule out the possibility of an explicitly religious interpretation of dream figures. For example, a dream figure of the Buddha might stand for compassion or Jesus might symbolize heroism or sacrificial love but these figures would not be interpreted as manifestations of God or the gods themselves. The humanistic perspective would also be unable to account for psychic dreams or those dreams that give information about the external world. The theoretical limits of humanistic psychology are less restrictive than classical psychoanalytic interpretations of explicit religion, nevertheless they do rule out an explicit religious interpretation of dream symbols where for instance the Buddha in a dream actually evokes the presence of Buddha.

On the other hand, the practice of Gestalt dream interpretation is less restrictive than the theoretical principles outlined by Fritz Perls. Because Gestalt places little value in "talking about" and therefore interpreting dream symbols, the theoretical restriction implicit in humanistic psychology does not greatly influence the actual process of Gestalt dream work. The theoretical principle that all parts of the dream represent aspects of the dreamer does not prevent the dreamer from enacting the roles of various dream figures in such a way that the religious meaning of those figures could still come through. In such a case we are dealing with implicit rather than explicit religion.[12]

In Fritz Perls' approach to Gestalt therapy, enacting a religious dream character might put the dreamer in touch with the meaning and experience of that religious character, but the mode of relationship would be *identification with* a spiritual force rather than *dialogue with* an independent spiritual force. The religious figure would speak *through* the dreamer rather than *to* the dreamer. Gestaltists would see no problem in this type of enactment since they assume that the religious dream figure is in reality a part of the dreamer's personality. The strategy of Gestalt dream work is, in fact, to identify with all elements of the dream. According to Perls, many mental disturbances are due to psychological fragmentation and the alienation of individuals from various aspects of their own psyche. Dreams provide a dramatic portrait of these "disowned" and projected parts which require integration.

Interpreting dreams at the subjective level where the dream represents the dreamer's present psychological state and way of being in the world is the primary characteristic of humanistic dream analysis. This approach to dreams is particularly productive in psychotherapy but it seldom reaches the level of an explicitly religious interpretation of dreams where the dreamer may encounter God or the spiritual world. To understand this explicitly religious level of dream interpretation more fully we turn to transpersonal psychology.

Notes

1. "Introduction," *Journal of Humanistic Psychology*, 1/1 (1961), vi-ix.
2. F. Perls: "In Gestalt Therapy we don't interpret dreams. We do something much more interesting with them. Instead of analyzing and further cutting up the dream, we want to bring it back to life." *Gestalt Therapy Verbatim*, p. 73.
3. *Gestalt Therapy Verbatim* (Maob, Utah, 1974), pp. 114-115.
4. The underline is in the text.
5. *Gestalt Therapy Verbatim*, p. 118.
6. In Gestalt therapy psychological disorders are seen primarily as interruptions in the free functioning of the organism as it satisfies its needs. These interruptions are termed contact-boundary disturbances because they occur at the point where the organism contacts the environment. The Gestalt method helps a person to become aware of *how* he or she interrupts the organism's creative adjustments to the environment. A person's dreams, body posture, gestures, or voice tone often reveal how and where these interruptions occur.
7. Perls states his view of dream work in these terms: "Now if my contention is correct, which I believe of course it is, all the different parts of the

dream are fragments of our personalities. Since our aim is to make everyone of us a wholesome person, which means a unified person without conflicts, what we have to do is put the different fragments of the dream together. We have to *re-own* these projected fragmented parts of our personality, and *re-own* the hidden potential that appears in the dream." *Gestalt Therapy Verbatim*, p. 71.

8. Integration refers to increased awareness of personality characteristics and a more harmonious interaction between them and the coexistence of various feelings, attitudes and ideas that constitute the dreamer's personality.

9. Janie Rhyne, "The Gestalt Art Experience," in *Gestalt Therapy Now*, eds. J. Fagan and I. Shepherd (New York, 1970), pp. 274-284.

10. Perls speaks about the educational value of group dream work in these terms: "I believe that in the workshop, you learn so much by understanding what's going on in this other person, and realize that so much of his conflicts are your own, and by identification you learn. Learning equals discovery. You discover yourself and awareness is the means of discovery." *Gestalt Therapy Verbatim*, pp. 77-78.

11. Humanistic psychology's tendency to interpret religious symbols as human potential can be seen in Erich Fromm's *Psychoanalysis and Religion* (New Haven, 1950), Gordon Allport's *The Individual and His Religion* (New York, 1960), and Abraham Maslow's *The Farther Reaches of Human Nature* (New York, 1970).

12. Implicit religion means a person's deepest values and world view, even if these are not connected with any ritual or mythical aspects of an organized religion. The sense of implicit religion could be involved with any of the general forces of psychology since everyone has a world view and holds some values whether or not they consciously reflect on them.

Transpersonal Psychology

Transpersonal psychology, sometimes called the Fourth Force in psychology, is in one sense the most recent general development in psychology. In another sense its roots go back to William James and Carl Jung and even to the ancient search for mystical experience and the Sacred. The name "transpersonal" refers to certain forces that influence human thinking, feeling and behavior and are not strictly the product of an individual's own personal psychology and conditioning. In the inaugural issue of the *Journal of Transpersonal Psychology*, the editor, Anthony Sutich, listed the concerns of transpersonal psychology. These include: ultimate values, unitive consciousness, peak experiences, ecstasy, mystical experience, awe, wonder, self-actualization, ultimate meaning, cosmic awareness, the sacralization of everyday life, transcendental phenomena, maximal sensory awareness, responsiveness and expression.[1] Transpersonal psychology studies how these experiences influence and transform human beings.

From the above list it is clear that there is some overlapping between transpersonal and humanistic psychology. Both are concerned with values, peak experiences, self-actualization and sensory awareness. Also, both view human life optimistically. Transpersonal tendencies toward ultimate states of being are assumed to be positive just as humanistic psychology sees the essential core of human nature as positive, or at least morally neutral. Therapy in transpersonal psychology tends to trust the creative, imaginative and mystical impulses of humans. This is like "uncovering" therapy in humanistic psychology that trusts human nature and seeks health in a release of human potential and in the self-regulating wisdom of the organism.

Sutich considers Abraham Maslow to be the prime mover of both humanistic and transpersonal psychology. The original editorial board of the *Journal of Transpersonal Psychology* also reflects the common heritage of both these psychological movements: Michael Murphy, Medard Boss, Victor Frankl,

Abraham Maslow, and Clark Moustakas—all important figures in humanistic psychology.

Transpersonal psychology reaches back beyond these contemporary psychologists to William James for its openness to transcendent and religious phenomena. James' attitude toward transcendent phenomena has a direct bearing on transpersonal dream interpretation even though he himself did not write much about dreams. Since his view of the human psyche allowed for the intrusion of the divine and the spirit world, he took seriously people's reports of religious experiences. He did not reduce these experiences to obsessions, wishes or psychological and physical dependencies as did Freud. Nor did he accept the viewpoint that religious experiences were merely the product of the nervous system, conditioning, age, hypnosis, psychopathology, psychic phenomena or subconscious activity.[2]

Another forerunner of transpersonal psychology is Carl Jung, whose Analytical Psychology is the longest-standing school of psychology devoted to the investigation of transpersonal phenomena. Jung is particularly important for us because dream interpretation lies at the center of his approach to the psyche. Since Jung's method exemplifies transpersonal dream interpretation we shall consider his approach in this section.

When interpreting dreams the first thing Jung noticed was the dramatic structure of the manifest dream. He attended to the actors and setting of a dream and to plot development. The crucial point in a dream is where a major change in the action occurs. Any plot resolution may indicate a solution to a problem or an alternative way of viewing a current situation or relationship in the dreamer's life.

After considering the dramatic structure Jung elicited associations to each element in the dream. Where Freud used free association to get at the meaning of the latent dream, Jung applied a method of directed association to discover a dream's meaning. Directed association means that the associations are all directed to a specific dream symbol embedded in a specific dream context. The manifest dream provides the interpretive context for directed association. For Jung the manifest dream is central. He did not accept Freud's view that the latent dream thoughts are the essential dream and that they are distorted and disguised in the manifest dream. For Jung the strange qualities of the manifest dream such as discontinuities, absurdities, transformations, condensations, displacements, etc. are merely characteristics of symbolic language; they are not distortions designed to hide a dream's meaning but are vehicles to communicate its meaning.

Directed association keeps the dream context in the forefront as the dreamer says what comes to mind in regard to each of the dream symbols. The dream itself sets limits to which associations illuminate the dream. Jung uses the term circumambulation (to walk around) to describe the dynamics of directed association: the dreamer keeps the dream setting in mind as she circles the dream symbol with her associations. So in the example of the dream with a horse galloping out of control toward a lake, associations would always return to that dream setting. The dreamer would recall any memories, feelings or attitudes about horses. These personal associations would offer the first clues to the meaning of the dream. If the dreamer remembers that she was once on a runaway horse, the dream may be comparing some present life circumstance with that earlier experience of danger.

If the dreamer is unable to come up with any personal associations to a dream image, then the dreamer or analyst may draw on cultural associations to shed light on the dream's meaning. In our culture horses may represent instincts, sexuality or some other force of nature so the horse in this dream may represent some instinct or drive that is out of control in the dreamer's life. In the event there are no personal or cultural associations to the dream image Jung would consider whether there is some myth in which a horse functions in a way similar to its role in this particular dream. Some mythical associations link horses to the blind forces of nature or magical powers and divination.[3]

Whether the associations are personal, cultural or archetypal the specific dream image and setting guide the dream interpretation. Whatever light the cultural or archetypal images may shed on the meaning of the horse, the interpretation must still account for this specific horse galloping out of control toward a lake.

Many assume that the archetypal level is the most important feature of Jungian dream analysis. In the everyday work of dream interpretation this is not the case. Personal associations take priority over the cultural and archetypal associations in determining a dream's meaning.[4] Archetypal associations are especially important where the dreamer has no associations at all to the dream images and where no cultural associations suggest themselves, but this happens infrequently.[5]

Jung, like Freud, considers the dreamer's life circumstances. The dreamer's present circumstances provide further context for interpreting a dream. This context helps to determine whether the dream figures refer to aspects of the dreamer's personality (the subjective level of interpretation) or to people in the external world (the objective level of interpretation).[6]

Jung also wanted to discover the compensatory function of a dream. Dreams add to the waking perspective a totally different point of view that compensates for the one-sided concentration of the waking mind. Where the waking mind focuses on adapting to present life circumstances, the timeless unconscious brings to the dreamer's attention all those aspects of life that were ignored because they had no bearing on present adaptation. So Jung would ask: What new perspective is this dream providing, or what is this dream compensating for in the conscious perspective or attitude of the dreamer?

Another aspect of Jung's method is active imagination, a technique designed to explore dream images in greater depth. In active imagination a person contemplates a dream image until it spontaneously begins to change or speak. The person should suspend a critical attitude that says: "Nothing will happen. The image won't change." An overly aesthetic concern with the quality or beauty of the image also interferes with active imagination. The correct attitude is to patiently contemplate the dream image and wait for it to move or speak.

Jung also paid special attention to the dream series in his method of interpretation.[7] He asked his patients to keep a careful record of their dreams. The more dreams commenting upon the dreamer's current situation, the greater the likelihood of correct interpretation. The dreams in a series are like the chapters of a book that contribute to the total story. Jung states his view this way:

> Every interpretation is an hypothesis, an attempt to read an unknown text. An obscure dream, taken in isolation, can hardly ever be interpreted with any certainty. For this reason I attach little importance to the interpretation of single dreams. A relative degree of certainty is reached only in the interpretation of a series of dreams, where the later dreams correct the mistakes we have made in handling those that went before. Also the basic ideas and themes can be recognized much better in a dream series . . .[8]

Jung sees the dream series as part of the context for interpreting a dream. For Jung the dream series is coherent and its overall meaning unfolds almost on its own.

Finally, Jung asked his analysands to develop certain dream themes by drawing, painting or sculpting them or by applying some other creative form of expression to dream images. Jung created this form of expanding on dreams through exploring his own dream images. This is a way to continue the dream and gain further insights into the meaning and reference of dream images. Jung emphasized that people should express symbols in this way not to create art but to understand a dream more fully.

We might summarize the elements in Jungian dream interpretation in the following chart:

Jungian Method

1) Notice the dramatic structure of the dream:
   a) persons, place and time on dream stage
   b) plot development
   c) climax of plot: major change in the action
   d) resolution of plot

2) Associate to each dream image:
   a) personal associations
   b) cultural associations
   c) mythical associations
3) Consider the dreamer's life situation.
4) Determine subjective or objective reference of the dream.
5) Consider how the dream compensates for the dreamer's waking point of view.
6) Use active imagination with various dream images.
7) Consider the dream series.
8) Give artistic expression to dream elements.

As noted earlier in this section, transpersonal psychology studies how certain types of experience transform human beings. Various religious traditions also speak of these transformations. They speak of humans encountering the divine and of being changed as a result of the encounter. Jung describes this transformation in a number of ways: the disappearance of I-ness, the emergence of the Self-archetype,[9] acquiring an attitude of attention to the numinous (the divine will), becoming whole, reconciling psychological opposites and discovering the myth that lives through the individual.

Some of these descriptions appear to be cast in religious terms, such as the emergence of the Self-archetype and acquiring an attitude of attention to the numinous which expresses the divine will. These two descriptions are similar to the traditional language of transformation as the encounter with God and the change resulting from that encounter. One reason why Jung is important to transpersonal psychology is his attention to ideas and symbols that have been excluded from consideration in other forms of psychology. In the following dreams of Jung we see how his interpretations go beyond the subjective level to transpersonal levels.

In *Memories, Dreams, Reflections* Jung discusses a couple of his dreams and visions that show his openness to interpreting dream images of the dead as possible spirit-world contacts. He describes a dream he had twice only six weeks after his father's death. His father appeared to him and said he was just returning from a holiday. Jung thought his father would be annoyed at him because he had moved into his father's room after his death. Jung says he felt ashamed in the dream because he had imagined his father was dead and actually the father was getting ready to come home again. There are clearly subjective elements involved in this dream since it may express his ambivalence toward his father and guilt about having taken over his dead father's room at home. Jung says it was an unforgettable experience that his dead father returned in a dream and seemed so real. He says it forced him for the first time to think about life after death.[10] This shows that Jung did entertain the possibility that the dream image of a dead person might actually bring the dreamer in contact with the dead person's spirit.

Jung recalls another dream that raised questions about interpreting dreams involving the dead or dying.[11] The night before Jung's mother died he had this frightening dream: He was in a dense primeval forest. Suddenly he heard a piercing whistle that made his knees shake and seemed to resound through the whole universe. A gigantic wolfhound burst from the underbrush. As it tore past him he suddenly knew that the Wild Huntsman had commanded the wolfhound to carry away a human soul. He awoke in terror. The next morning he received news that his mother died.

Jung interprets this dream along archetypal lines, seeing the Wild Huntsman as Wotan, the god of his forefathers, who took his mother back to her ancestors. Although Christianity saw Wotan as a devil, he was an important nature spirit who symbolized the goal of the alchemists. For Jung the dream says that his mother's soul was taken into the wholeness of nature, a territory beyond Christian morality.

Here again Jung's interpretation is not limited to the subjective level. He recognizes that the dream is operating at the archetypal level of universal images, connecting him with an ancient tradition of a spirit world and life after death. As he continues to comment on this dream he speaks of a viewpoint that is beyond the ego's assessment of death. From this perspective death is a joyful event, a wedding. Here it seems that Jung is speaking not merely of an archetypal pattern of imaging about his mother's death but at least potentially of the experience and fate of his mother's soul. Also there is a telepathic or clair-voyant element to this dream which involves seeing his mother's death at a place some distance away from where she died.

In another psychic dream involving his mother's death we see Jung interpreting the dream at the precognitive, archetypal and spirit-world levels.[12] In this dream Jung's long-dead father appears to him as if he had returned from a long journey. In the dream Jung was looking forward to finding out what his father had been up to and telling his father about his own life in recent years. But his father was preoccupied with marital psychology and he wanted to learn form Jung about the complexities of marriage.

Jung interprets this dream as a forecast of his mother's death since his father showed up after an absence of twenty-six years to learn the latest insights on marital problems. Jung sees this as his father preparing to resume in the after-life the marital relationship with his dying mother. Jung concludes that in the timeless state of the spirit world his father had gained no more understanding of marriage and therefore needed a living person, whose knowledge grew with the changed times, to provide him with guidance. Jung says that he could discover more about the dream by considering its subjective meaning, but he remains fascinated with the precognitive and spirit-world levels of inter-pretation. Here he reiterates his view of psychological relativity wherein the unconscious can know the future because it is ex-tended forward in time while the conscious mind is limited to here-and-now sense perceptions. He also considers the value of the mythic dream images that illuminate the spirit world. Jung feels that we are dependent on small hints from dreams and other unconscious material for our understanding of life after death.

When Jung singles out such dreams from a life-time of remembered dreams we can be certain they are profoundly im-portant for his understanding of dreams. In these examples Jung is primarily concerned with transpersonal levels of dream interpretation.[13] While he does not doubt the value of the sub-jective meaning of dreams, here he goes beyond the subjective level to consider the archetypal, psychic and spirit-world dimensions of dreams.

Of the four major forces of psychology considered in this chapter, transpersonal psychology appears to offer the most effective paradigm for dream interpretation in the psychology of religion. In the last chapter we shall see how the major forces of psychology have influenced dream interpretation in the psychology of religion as we consider rules for interpreting dreams, but first I want to situate dream interpretation more explicitly in the psychology of religion.

Notes

1. "Introduction," *Journal of Transpersonal Psychology,* 1/1 (1969), i.
2. James elaborates his method in *The Varieties of Religious Experience* (New York, 1958), chs. 1 and 2.
3. J.E. Cirlot, *A Dictionary of Symbols* (New York, 1962), pp. 144-45.
4. J. Hall, "Dream Interpretation in Analysis," in *Jungian Analysis* (LaSalle, Illinois, 1982), pp. 141, 143 and 151.
5. It is also possible for a symbol to operate at two or three levels at once. In the "Snakes and Ladder" dream in chapter four, associations to the snake symbol are personal, cultural and archetypal.
6. "If, therefore, I dream of a person with whom I am connected by a vital interest, the interpretation on the objective level will certainly be nearer to the truth than the other. But if I dream of a person who is not important to me in reality, then interpretation on the subjective level will be nearer to the truth." "General Aspects of Dream Psychology," *CW* 8, p. 267.
7. Jung published some valuable examples of interpreting the dream series: *Symbols of Transformation (CW 5)*, "Individual Dream Symbolism in Relation to Alchemy" *(CW* 12, pp. 39-223), and *The Visions Seminars* (Zuerich, 1976).
8. Jung, "The Practical Use of Dream Analysis," *CW* 16, p. 150.
9. The Self-archetype is seen by Jungians as the regulator of the entire psyche, conscious and unconscious.
10. Jung, *Memories, Dreams, Reflections* (New York, 1965), pp. 96-97.
11. *Ibid.,* p. 313.
12. *Ibid.,* p. 315.
13. For another example of transpersonal dream interpretation in the psychology of religion see "A Childhood Dream" in my study: *Flesh as Transformation Symbol in the Theology of Anselm of Canterbury: Historical and Transpersonal Perspectives* (Lewiston, N.Y., 1985), pp. 25-32.

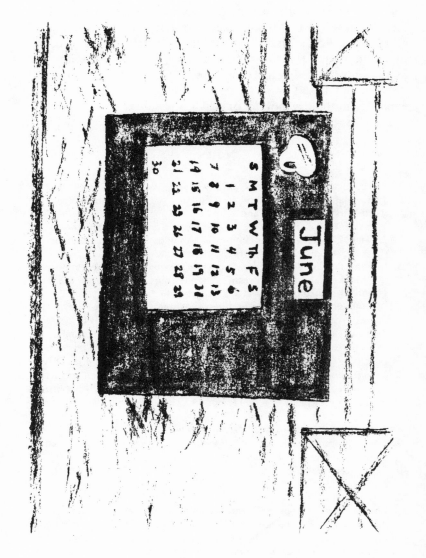

Dream Illustration No. 1

"The Ring in June"

I'm visiting a friend. There is another man there also as a guest, a Professor Luna. The three of us and my friend's little boy walk out to their barn. The professor tells the boy a fairy tale and when he finishes he gives me a present. The gift is rolled up. As I open it I'm not sure whether it is a picture or a calendar. When I look more closely I see that it is a shiny blue calendar. In the upper left-hand corner there is a symbol, a silver and gold ring. It seems to be commemorating the day I visit someone though it's not clear whom I'm to visit. I say "That is a ring of power." As I study the calendar I marvel at how beautiful this present is. My friend says he likes the calendar very much and would hang it in his home.

This dream occured on May 23rd, 1981, one month before my father died. I was unable to make much sense of it at the time and decided to do a water color of the calendar in the hope that some associations might emerge. Nothing occured to me as I did the picture. Two weeks after this I went to see my father in Florida as he was deteriorating rapidly from cancer after a ten-year struggle. On the day I arrived a friend and I took my father into the hospital. In the hospital he gave me the silver and gold ring he was wearing. A week and a half later, on June 24th, he died.

Some weeks after the funeral when I was back in Toronto I remembered my dream "The Ring in June." I checked the picture I had painted then and noticed that one or two dates were missing from the calendar. The 23rd and the 25th are not clearly drawn. The 24th is definitely missing in the calendar painting though I do not recall all details of how the calendar looked in the dream. The drawing does not represent dream precognition, but it did produce a striking coincidence. The picture says symbolically that the day my father dies normal time will stop or will not exist for me. The dream painting seems to know a month in advance the time of my father's death and to use the symbol of "missing time" to portray my psychological state in that disturbing period.

It is also significant to me that a Professor Luna gives me the calendar since "luna" means moon and is a symbol of the unconscious and time. The dream seems to be saying that this symbolic calendar is a gift from the unconscious. In the dream I say, "That is a ring of power." This refers to Carlos Castaneda's expression for the kind of attention that imparts order to different types of reality. For me the "ring of power" is associated with non-ordinary reality, a state where normal time stops and the future can be seen as present. Both of these phenomena do occur in the dream world. In this case, normal time is suspended in the calendar painting where the day of my father's death is missing and my future visit to my father is marked by the dream ring he gave me upon entering the hospital. For me these meaningful coincidences make this dream and the events following it particularly memorable. This uncanny dream experience compelled me to contemplate a transpersonal source of wisdom which knows something about my future life.

Chapter III

Dreams in the Psychology of Religion

The psychology of religion deals with the psychological study of the many different aspects of religion including religious experience, mystical experience, human transformation and dreams. Here I shall briefly review some of the main lines of development within the psychology of religion that have a bearing on dream interpretation.[1]

William James, the great pioneer in the psychology of religion, set out to define the parameters of this discipline almost ninety years ago. While he did not deal extensively with dreams, he did establish certain emphases that give context to dream interpretation in the psychology of religion. In *The Varieties of Religious Experience*,[2] his ground-breaking lectures delivered in Edinburough, Scotland, in 1901, he established the principal categories in the psychology of religion and the primary importance of religious experience as the central focus of study.

James' working definition of religion highlights feelings and experience and downplays institutional, doctrinal and ritual factors. He defined religion as the "feelings, acts, and experiences of individual men in their solitude, so far as they apprehend themselves to stand in relation to whatever they may consider divine."[3] While this definition is very individualistic and reflects the perspective of liberal Protestantism, it has shaped the primary standpoint of the psychology of religion from the beginning and continues to guide research in this discipline.

James' main categories of religious experience are:

1. the reality of the unseen (experiences of an unseen order of being);
2. Healthy-minded religious experience (the tendency to look upon things as good);
3. the sick (suffering) soul experience (the view that evil is the very essence of life);
4. conversion
5. saintliness
6. mysticism

While some of the names of these religious experiences and states of consciousness have changed over the years, the range of phenomena covered by these categories still remains fairly comprehensive and useful, especially in the approach of depth psychology to the psychology of religion.[4] Certain of these categories such as the reality of the unseen and mysticism can include various dream phenomena.

More important than James' classification of religious experience is his method of handling these phenomena. If we consider *The Varieties of Religious Experience* we see how he deals with various cases. His material comes from historical records, from biographical and autobiographical sources, from interviews, from the *Journal for Psychical Research*, from friends, and in one case, even from his own religious experience.[5] His primary concern in each of these cases is to discover the meaning that religious experience has for people.

James first considers the context of the religious experience. He notes the diverse attendant phenomena that surround many religious experiences. In a couple of cases he calls attention to hallucinations that frequently occur with certain types of religious experience.[6] In another circumstance he describes a psychic event that occurs with the experience.[7] The first step toward understanding religious experience focuses on a careful description of what is happening in the experience.

Next James notes collateral phenomena, i.e. what other

conditions or states of mind a particular experience might be like.[8] Sometimes a religious experience can be classified along with certain neurological disorders;[9] at other times it may be like certain forms of subconscious activity;[10] and occasionally it may resemble types of psychopathology.[11] Here James, the medical doctor, casts a critical eye on the variety of religious experiences he describes. Yet while he is aware of how frequently religious experiences resemble such things as neurological disorders, psychic events, trance states and even psychopathology, he does not automatically explain away these religious experiences as "nothing but neurological disorders" or "nothing but psychopathology." How does James manage to avoid the temptation to reduce religious phenomena to something else?

A brief answer to this question is found in James' phenomenological and pragmatic emphases. He evaluates the worth of religious experience according to two criteria: 1) what it means to the person who has it and 2) how it works in the person's life. For James it is neither the accompanying phenomena nor even the origins of the experience that are of primary concern in the psychology of religion. Rather he focuses on the inner meaning and the spiritual consequences that these experiences have for a person. Here he adopts an approach that anticipates the phenomenological method; he suspends judgment on what constitutes the essence of the experience and concentrates on what the experience means to the person who has it. For example, he would focus less on the question "Is this person having an hallucination or is she encountering God?" and more on a detailed description of the experience and how it relates to her view of the world and values in life.

Already we see here something of the other major characteristic of James' approach, namely his pragmatism. We might refer to this aspect of his method as a pragmatic concern for the consequences of religious experience. The crucial question is: How does the experience make a difference in the person's life? Some of these spiritual consequences are that the person experiences strength of soul, exercises charity and becomes aware of a wider life than that of the world's selfish interests. Here James goes back to the empiricist criterion: "By their fruits ye shall know them, not by their roots."[12]

So James understood the psychology of religion in such a way that the inner meaning of religious experience is central. Dreams may shed light on that inner meaning or even provide religious experiences. He also developed a non-reductive method of analysis that can guide dream interpretation in the psychology of religion. An example of how James would apply his non-reductive method to dreams can be found in his own profound, though unsystematic examination of a dream experience he had in 1906.

James originally reported these dreams in an article entitled "A Suggestion About Mysticism."[13] As an indication of how important this dream experience is for him, he introduces it as the most "intensely peculiar experience of my whole life."[14] While he states that these dreams and the experiences surrounding them may not constitute a mystical experience they do raise questions about the nature of dream reality and our possible relationship to one who may be dreaming our existence. Here is James' account of this remarkable dream experience.

San Francisco, Feb. 14th 1906.—The night before last, in my bed at Stanford University, I woke at 7:30 A.M., from a quiet dream of some sort, and whilst "gathering my waking wits," seemed suddenly to get mixed up with reminiscences of a dream of an entirely different sort, which seemed to telescope, as it were, into the first one, a dream very elaborate, of lions, and tragic. I concluded this to have been a previous dream of the same sleep; but the apparent mingling of two dreams was something very queer, which I had never before experienced.

On the following night (Feb. 12-13) I awoke suddenly from my first sleep, which appeared to have been very heavy, in the middle of a dream, in thinking of which I became suddenly confused by the contents of two other dreams that shuffled themselves abruptly in between the parts of the first dream, and of which I couldn't grasp the origin. Whence come *these dreams?* I asked. They were close to *me*, and fresh, as if I had just dreamed them; and yet they were far away *from the first dream.* The contents of the three had absolutely no connection. One had a cockney atmosphere, it had happened to someone in London. The other two were American. One involved the trying on of a coat (was this the dream I seemed to wake from?) the other was a sort of nightmare and had to do with soldiers. Each had a wholly distinct emotional atmosphere that made its individuality discontinuous with that of the others. And yet, in a moment, as these three dreams alternately telescoped into and out of each other, and I seemed to myself to have been their common dreamer, they seemed quite as distinctly *not* to have been dreamed in succession, in that one sleep. *When*, then? Not on a previous night, either. *When*, then, and *which* was the one out of which I had just awakened? *I could no longer tell:* one was as close to me as the others, and yet they entirely repelled each other, and I seemed thus to belong to three different dream-systems at once, no one of which would connect itself either with the others or with my waking life. I began to feel curiously confused and *scared*, and tried to wake myself up wider, but I seemed already wide-awake. Presently cold shivers of dread ran over me: *Am I getting into other people's dreams?* Is this a "telepathic" experience? Or an invasion of double (or treble) personality? Or is it a thrombus in a cortical artery? and the beginning of a general mental "confusion" and disorientation which is going on to develop who knows how far?

Decidedly I was losing hold of my "self," and making acquaintance with a quality of mental distress that I had never known before, its nearest analogue being the sinking, giddying anxiety that one may have when, in the woods, one discovers that one is really "lost." Most human troubles look towards a terminus. Most fears point in a direction and concentrate towards a climax. Most assaults of the evil one may be met by bracing oneself against something, one's principles, one's courage, one's will, one's pride. But in this experience all was diffusion from a centre, and foothold swept away, the brace itself disintegrating all the faster as one needed its support more direly. Meanwhile vivid perception (or remembrance) of the various dreams kept coming over me in alternation. Whose? *whose? WHOSE? Unless I can attach* them, I am swept out to sea with no horizon and no bond, getting *lost*.

The idea aroused the "creeps" again, and with it the fear
of again falling asleep and renewing the process. It had
begun the previous night, but then the confusion had only
gone one step, and had seemed simply curious. *This* was
the second step—where might I be after a third step had
been taken?[15]

James interpreted the form of these dreams more than he
did the content. The few dream elements he reveals are that on
February 13th one was set in London, the other two in the
States, one was a nightmare with soldiers, and another was
about trying on a coat and on February 12th there was an
elaborate, tragic dream with lions. With only these dream contents as well as feelings of dread and mental distress to go on,
the typical methods of dream interpretation described in
chapter two do not shed much light on James' troubling dream
experience.

The meaning of these dreams will remain mere speculation
without knowing more about James' immediate life context at
the time of the dream and his own associations to the images.
Even when a dream touches upon the deepest layers of the
psyche, the archetypal images produced relate to the particular
situation which activates them. In the Jungian view, these profound dream images may be compensating for some one-
sidedness in the conscious standpoint. Perhaps it was the element of tragedy that the unconscious was highlighting as James
approached death. He had known since 1898 that he had heart
disease and it was a losing battle. It may be that James' conscious mind was blocking the sense of tragedy in seeing his own
extraordinary life nearing its end. Could "trying on a coat"
refer to the identity transformation involved in dying?

Apart from any such speculation on the dream content, we
should consider James' own struggle with the discontinuous and
fragmented form of the dreams. Their startlingly different
atmosphere and character bewildered James. They were so different from each other he suspects that some of them may have
been dreamed by a different person. He wonders whose dream
fragments he may be receiving through a telepathic dream
network.

At the heart of his confusion lies his experience of belonging to three different dream systems at once. It occurs to him he may be experiencing three different personalities within himself at the same time without any unifying thread of identity. Mixing together these different levels of psychic life is like getting lost in the woods for James. The normal thread of continuity that characterizes waking identity is largely a construct of the ego and in this situation his ego fails to assert its unifying activity. James worries that this experience may represent a deterioration of his mind. His understanding of the psyche allows for separate aspects of personality to coexist as idea groups centered around an aim.[16] He also recognizes how these idea groups can conflict and create a divided self, an experience that is extremely troubling and often preceeds conversion.[17] Autonomous activity of these idea groups might account for his upsetting dream experience.

James' strategy for dealing with his confusion is to try to make himself more wide-awake, to break the illusion of the disturbing dream reality by stepping up ego activity. He attempts to tame or transform his anxiety by entering into his customary and grounded perspective: the scientific observer. He hopes these dreams may provide experience and insight into possibilities which he previously studied and only accounted for theoretically.

In *The Principles of Psychology* James speaks of multiple realities created and maintained by our interest and attention.[18] Getting into other people's dreams suggests the possibility that dreams belong to a separate reality that we can share. For James the subliminal region is where dreams emerge and where the divine or other spiritual realities may enter. He describes how the subconscious may be the region where psychological experience and religious experience meet.[19] While James confesses that he himself never had a religious experience in the classical form described by mystics, in his book *The Varieties* he did include his panic fear attack and his experiences with nitrous oxide as examples of religious experiences.[20] We should also remember that he discusses these strange dreams in an article entitled "A Suggestion About Mysticism." Although James knows that pathological elements may be involved in the formation of these dreams, nevertheless he sees their mystical potential. There is no evidence of an explicitly religious interpretation of these dream images, but he does relate their bizarre *form* to the possibility that they were dreamed by a mysterious stranger. This mysterious being may represent the divine or beings of the spiritual realm.

As the scientific observer, James halts his mystical "drift" out of "his customary self." He objectifies and distances himself from his identity confusion and gradually calms himself. He continues to reflect on this disturbing experience:

> Evidently I was in full possession of my reflective wits; and whenever I thus objectively thought of the situation in which I was, my anxieties ceased. But there was a tendency to relapse into the dreams and reminiscences, and to relapse vividly; and then the confusion recommenced, along with the emotion of dread lest it should develop farther.[21]

Still he is in danger of falling back into his dream confusion so he struggles again to reestablish his waking ego solidly in the here and now. He locates himself in the midnight hour, ever the relentless investigator, now wondering about the difference between midnight dreams and those dreamed after 2:00 a.m.:

> Half-past twelve! Midnight, therefore. And this gave me another reflective idea. Habitually, on going to bed, I fall into a very deep slumber from which I never naturally awaken until after two. I never awaken, therefore, from a midnight dream, as I did tonight, so of midnight dreams my ordinary consciousness retains no recollection. My sleep seemed terribly heavy as I woke to-night. Dream states carry dream memories—why may not the two succedaneous dreams (whichever two of the three *were* succedaneous) be memories of *twelve o'clock dreams of previous nights*, swept in, along with the just-fading dream, into the just-waking system of memory? Why, in short, may I not be tapping in a way precluded by my ordinary habit of life, *the mid-night stratum* of my past experiences?

> This idea gave great relief—I felt now as if I were in
> full possession of my *anima rationalis* . . .[22]

Whether or not this was a mystical dream experience James
seems extremely relieved to have worked himself through it.
Had this experience preceded His Edinborough lectures I
imagine he would have included it under the "sick (suffering)
soul" variety of religious experience. While James' wrestling
with these dreams does not represent a systematic dream interpretation, it does exhibit his open-mindedness about the
possibility of various dream realities, including a reality that
could intimately relate humans to God. At the end of his discussion of these dreams James offers this advice about the
psychological investigation of such phenomena:

> The ordinary psychologist disposes of the phenomena (the
> mystical uncovering of tracts of consciousness) under the
> conveniently "scientific" head of *petit mal*, if not of
> "bosh" or "rubbish." But we know so little of the noetic
> value of abnormal mental states of any kind that in my
> own opinion we had better keep an open mind and collect
> facts sympathetically for a long time to come. We shall not
> understand these alterations of consciousness either in this
> generation or in the next.[23]

The most fruitful research on dreams in the psychology of
religion heeds James' advice and recognizes the limitations of
our knowledge about the spiritual potential of dreams. Now I
would like to sketch how some psychologists since James have
contributed to the study of dreams in the psychology of
religion.

The Four Forces in the Psychology of Religion

Experimental Psychology of Religion

I have already mentioned how in the early years of its development psychology (especially experimental psychology and behaviorism) treated religious experience as a concern of unenlightened times or an expression of mental illness rather than as a phenomenon to be studied seriously. In the 1960's this attitude was challenged by a number of experimental psychologists who attempted to bring meditation and mysticism into the laboratory. Many of the studies in Charles Tart's volume *Altered States of Consciousness* exemplify this fresh interest in the psychology of religion as considered from the experimental vantage point.[24]

The advantage of the experimental approach is that it quantifies and statistically analyzes the data to determine its significance. It is able to isolate individual factors in order to explore how they work in detail. Using a control group also helps to determine whether the results of an experimental group are genuinely significant. The disadvantage of the experimental method in psychology of religion is that it is limited to what is measurable while these factors often are not crucial for understanding the most profound aspects of religious experience. Students often question whether experiments in this area shed much light on the nature of religion, and especially on their own experience of religion.

Experimental design and analysis in the psychology of religion appear to be improving. Recent works in this area indicate some fruitful directions for future research but unfortunately they do not deal with dreams. However, two areas of experimental psychology which promise to shed light on dreams in psychology of religion are dream content analysis and lucid dream research. In chapter two I focused on Calvin Hall's dream content analysis so here I shall discuss the experimental research of Stephen LaBerge at the Stanford University Sleep Research Center.

LaBerge is an experimental psychologist who investigates lucid dreaming in the sleep laboratory. He was able to demonstrate conditions that underlie lucid dreaming by monitoring the sleep of people who were proficient lucid dreamers. These dreamers agreed that they would give a pre-arranged signal when they became lucid in a dream. When they became aware that they were dreaming and gave this signal, the EEG reading and rapid eye movements indicated that they were in fact in REM sleep. Lucid dreamers underwent all of the physiological changes characteristic of REM sleep described in chapter two. These studies made it clear that lucid dreaming is not just a form of day dreaming or imagination as people had previously speculated. Lucid dreams are definitely a product of the REM dream state.

LaBerge deals with many applications for lucid dreaming, from their potential in psychotherapy to their role in creativity. He reflects on the theoretical and spiritual implications of his research in a way that also contributes to transpersonal psychology. LaBerge proposes a means whereby we can explore in the laboratory certain religious and metaphysical questions which relate to dreaming. In his discussion of "shared dreams" he considers the objective character of the dream state. "Shared dreams" refer to the situation where two or more people claim to have identical dreams on the same night. Such dreams suggest that the dream sharers have in fact been together in the same dream world. This implies that the dream world and the people in it possess some kind of objective existence.

Here is a laboratory experiment LaBerge proposes to test whether two people can actually share each other's dream:

> Two oneironauts could have simultaneous lucid dreams while being monitored in a sleep laboratory. They would agree to meet in their lucid dreams and signal simultaneously. If the experience were truly a mutual dream—that is, if the lucid dreamers are actually sharing a dream world—simultaneous eye-movement signals would show up in their polygraph recordings. If, on the other hand, they reported carrying out this task in a mutual lucid dream but did not show simultaneous signals, we should

have to conclude that they were at most sharing dream plots . . . However, if they did produce simultaneous eye-movement signals, we have incontrovertable proof for the objective existence of the dream world. We would then know that, in certain circumstances at least, dreams can be as objectively real as the world of physics. This would finally raise the question of whether physical reality is itself some kind of mutual dream.[25]

LaBerge has not yet attempted this experiment, but it has fascinating possibilities.

LaBerge also describes lucid dreaming as it is carried out in yoga.[26] Here the goal is to awaken from the illusion of this existence through a process of lucid dreaming. First the dreamer strives to comprehend the nature of the dream state by becoming proficient at lucid dreaming. The yogi learns to control his reactions to the contents of his lucid dreams and becomes able to visit any realm of existence in dreams. Then he comes to realize that the dream state is *maya* (illusion). The yogi practices the art of transforming dream content and gradually sees that his own dream body is just as much an illusion as the other elements in his lucid dream. Finally, by meditating on the fact that what he sees in dreams as "deities" are actually his own mental images, he is able to keep his mind free of thought. In this state the Clear Light dawns. The yogi eventually realizes that everything perceived in the waking state is equally as unreal as what he experiences in the dream state since waking and dreaming are both states of mind.[27]

LaBerge reflects upon the implications of lucid dreaming as a spiritual path. For him the danger of this path to realization is "psychic inflation." The inexperienced dreamer may misinterpret control over lucid dreams to mean that he or she is actually the originator of dreams or the true self—what Jung speaks of as the Self archetype or the God-image. This is the temptation to imagine you are the God who is the author of your dreams and who appears in your dreams. But LaBerge trusts that the "fully lucid dreamer" will recognize that the dream ego is just another dream figure and not one's true self. He says that the fully lucid dream is a "transcendental experience" that helps to detach us from fixed ideas about ourselves.[29]

While lucid dreamers are likely at first to seek fulfillment of ego drives and desires, they may soon tire of such effortless gratification and relinquish deliberate dream control. LaBerge speaks of this as a surrender that might be phrased by traditionally religious people as "submission to the will of God" or by others as "giving control to your true self" or "surrender to the Highest."[30] He does not enter into the question of whether this "Highest" is part of yourself or something beyond yourself. Even when lucid dreamers give up controlling the course of their dreams, they can continue to use lucidity to respond to whatever happens in the dream and to follow the intentions of a higher will.

When LaBerge discusses the theoretical and spiritual implications of his experimental research, he shows himself to be open-minded in the Jamesian tradition of the psychology of religion. He does not rule out the possibility that dreams may place the dreamer in contact with a transcendent reality. LaBerge's viewpoint is in sharp contrast to Calvin Hall's, another experimental psychologist. Hall states: "Dreams are not mysterious, supernatural or esoteric phenomena. They are not messages from the gods nor are they prophecies of the future."[31] Hall does not allow for the possibility that dreams may refer to or evoke transcendent spiritual realities. This stems not from any conclusion based on empirical data but rather is an *a priori* judgment and thus would seem to limit the relevance of his content analysis to the psychology of religion.

While Hall himself does not leave much room for a religious interpretation of dreams, we should not link his personal viewpoint too closely to the creative method of dream analysis which he originated. His experimental method has potential to shed light on religious elements that appear in dreams. For example, content analysis could highlight the frequency of certain religious symbols in dreams, such as religious characters (Moses, Buddha, Jesus, Mohammed, the saints, etc.), religious buildings (churches, synagogues, mosques, temples, shrines), or religious objects (the cross, garments for religious rituals, the mandala, etc.). These symbols could be correlated with other characteristics of these groups or individuals to determine what connections there are in the unconscious between religious symbols and certain forms of behavior, attitudes, thoughts or feelings.

Because content analysis deals with a large number of dreams, it could also facilitate comparisons of religious dream symbols between various cultures and religious groups. Such an overview might suggest quantitative differences in the frequencies of certain kinds of religious symbols, but it would not necessarily illuminate the religious meaning of individual dreams. Since content analysis does not work with the dreamer's associations to dream symbols, it does not offer much help for interpreting any particular dream containing religious symbols. In this regard we might expect that psychoanalysis would be more useful in understanding the religious meaning of individual dreams since Freud developed the principal method of association to get at the underlying *meaning* of a dream.

Psychoanalytic Psychology of Religion

Although Freud developed a method that gets at the inner meaning of dreams, he did not leave room for an explicitly religious interpretation of dreams. Freud dealt with religion in a number of his works and we know that he had a good deal of religious training in his early life, in both primary and secondary school.[32] While he received highest possible marks for religion in his last year of secondary school and became a life-long friend of Sammuel Hammerschlag, his religion teacher, by the end of secondary school Freud declared himself an atheist.[33]

Freud's psychology of religion is comprehensive in scope, dealing at one time or another with all the major dimensions of religion such as ritual, myth, ethics, doctrine, religious experience and religious groups. Even though he did attend to all of these aspects of religion, he was one-sided in perspective. He also devoted the least amount of attention to that vital area of the psychology of religion which William James considered primary, namely, religious experience.

In *Totem and Taboo* he interprets religion as an obsessional neurosis.[34] Here Freud sees religion as rooted in guilt because the sons of the primal horde joined together to kill their father.[35] In *The Future of an Illusion* Freud sees religion as an illusion, that is, an idea derived from human wishes. He says religion is generated by our longing for the protection of a father to combat our anxiety in the face of human suffering, privation, nature's terrors and death.[36] In *Civilization and Its Discontents* Freud sees religious mystical experience as a regression to the stage of primary narcissism, the earliest phase of ego feeling where the individual is not yet differentiated from the environment and thus feels a sense of oneness with the world.[37]

In all of his works on the psychology of religion[38] Freud's view is consistently negative but his approach has had some constructive effects by purging religion of its more regressive elements. He made us more aware of the obsessional tendencies in certain private religious ceremonies. In *Group Psychology and the Analysis of the Ego* he helped to explain the religious cruelty and intolerance which has been such a scandal in the history of religions. He showed how religious ideas often reflect human wishes for personal gain more than genuine concern for seeing and doing the divine will. He also reminded us how infallible doctrines may discourage critical thinking and impoverish intelligence. In the area of ethics he pointed out how religion frequently leads to guilt complexes by sanctifying and absolutizing rules of conduct. And he explained how religious experience may be an attempt to escape responsibility for improving the world by regressing to infantile attitudes and feelings. In all of these ways Freud contributed to a more self-critical attitude about how religion may actually function in specific negative situations. Yet in regard to dreams, he ruled out a religious interpretation of symbols so that his approach does not shed much direct light on dreams in the psychology of religion.

Other psychoanalysts have been more open to religion however even their interpretation would exclude interpreting religious figures in dreams as actual spirits or symbols of the divine. To sketch the broad lines of development of the psychoanalytic approach since Freud three major trends can be discerned. These are the developments of ego psychology, object relations and self psychology.[39] We shall briefly consider each of these developments in relation to the psychology of religion.

Ego psychology originated in Freud's investigation of the ego's processes of repression.[40] Anna Freud, Franz Alexander, Heinz Hartmann and Erik Erikson are some of the important figures in this development of psychoanalysis. Perhaps the psychoanalyst who has contributed most to the psychology of religion has been Erikson.[41] His much heralded work in the area of religion, *Young Man Luther*, is an open-minded study of the great religious reformer which shows how Luther arrived at his identity through religious struggles. According to Erikson's theory of human development young people search for an ideology, i.e. a view of the world that helps them make sense of life. They often find at least part of their identity and worldview in religion. In his evaluation of the religious aspects of identity Erikson is much more sympathetic to the role of religion in human experience than was Freud. Erikson does not reduce religious phenomena to regressive sexual or aggressive drives, rather he holds that religion furthers our understanding and experience of the light and dark aspects of human existence.[42] Erikson also stresses the importance of pre-oedipal experience for later religious attitudes. The first contact with the mother is where an infant develops the basic trust that undergirds later religious development.

Erikson's writing on dreams reflects the care and empathy that characterize his work generally. Unlike orthodox Freudian analysts he highlights the importance of the manifest dream and shows how dreams reflect the ego's style of decision-making and its attitude toward life, problems and the world.[43] Though he tends to interpret dreams within the larger framework of his developmental theory of the "eight ages of man."[44] he is also aware of the important religious themes that have been portrayed in certain Indian tribes. In *Childhood and Society* he discusses the role of dreams in the Sioux Indian vision quest.[45]

He describes how the Sioux used dreams to guide vocations, hunting and warring as well as to bring innovations such as new songs, dances and prayers to the tribe. Even though he recognizes these spiritual aspects of dreams among North American Indians, he does not apply such explicit religious dream interpretation in his own psychoanalytic work. For example, in his reflection on William James' "mystical dream" Erikson interprets the dream as an identity problem in James' old-age despair[46] rather than as a mystical illumination of the nature of reality, which was part of James' own interpretation of his dream experience.

Here I shall also mention the work of Herbert Fingarette, a philosopher who has been greatly influenced by analytic ego psychology. In his work, *The Self in Transformation*, he discusses the view that dreams reveal another reality and may be related to Radhakrishnan's description of the subtle body and reincarnation. Such an interpretation would see the experiences portrayed in the manifest dream as eruptions of other lives into our present life experience.

Fingarette also notes that the Plains Indians treat the manifest dream as real incidents for which the dreamer is morally responsible and that Papuans converted to Catholicism sometimes confess adultery which they committed in dreams. Fingarette comments that "the dream is real life but not quite the same life as the day-life."[47] When he cites Baudelaire's view that the dream is potentially a genuine spiritual experience he seems to recognize the possibility of an explicitly religious interpretation of dreams. Although he does not elaborate on these suggestive ideas or clearly indicate how he would incorporate them into his own understanding of dreams, he does present these religious interpretations of dreams with considerable empathy.

In the second development of psychoanalytic thought, object relations theory, there is little attention to the role of religion. Object relations theory has its roots in the work of Melanie Klein and is represented by such figures as W.R. Fairbairn, Donald Winnicott, Harry Guntrip and Otto Kernberg.[48] They focus on the internalization of social relationships and how these relations affect normal and abnormal ego and super-ego development.[49] In these thinkers the healthy personal self is established especially in a good mother-infant relationship and meaningful relationship replaces adaptation of the ego as the therapeutic goal. "Replacement therapy" aims to give the basic security-giving relationship that mother did not provide.[50]

This psychoanalytic school has little room for a religious interpretation of dreams. John McDargh's *Psychoanalytic Object Relations Theory and the Study of Religion* is an exception to this general neglect of religion in object relations theory. He maintains that the object representation of God is one of the most significant in a person's life. McDargh's work considers only a few dreams, none with specifically religious imagery. While he does not highlight an explicitly religious interpretation, he is sensitive to the spiritual implications of overcoming a fragmented and underdeveloped self. Object relations analysts consider dreams mostly, if not entirely, as reliving emotional problems in human relationships.[51] To the degree that such problems reflect personal values and worldview, they may involve implicit religion. This line of enquiry is not underscored in object relations theory, nor do these theorists deal with an explicitly religious interpretation of dreams.

The third stream of psychoanalytic development, the self psychology of Heinz Kohut, has also had negligible impact on the psychology of religion. Kohut does see some value in religion in that conjuring up the presence of an idealized Godhead may allow people to act with great courage.[52] Kohut criticized Freud for ignoring this positive and supportive aspect of religion and he notes cases where the vision or voice of God has contributed to highly ethical and spiritual behavior.[53] He even recognizes the possibility of prophetic dreams but generally he does not interpret dreams in an explicitly religious way.[54] Rather he sees dreams as expressing the changes between the self and its relationship to the world.

Kohut has developed the notion of "self-state" dreams which "attempt to deal with the psychological danger by covering nameless processes with namable visual imagery."[55] In these dreams the manifest content reveals the meaning of the dream just as in the case of childhood and traumatic dreams. While such attention to the manifest dream is more likely to lead to an explicitly religious interpretation of dreams, Kohut himself does not usually move in that direction. We discover an exception, however, in his openness to some "dreams from above." About these unusual dreams he says:

> The contributions from the unconscious . . . do not determine the dream, and their uncovering would not give us the dream's essential meaning. It follows that we are, in such instances, not dependent on the free associations of the dreamer but can trust the dreamer's, generally unambiguously given, own explanation.[56]

Here Kohut focuses on the manifest dream in a way that leads to a transpersonal, explicitly spiritual, interpretation of these "dreams from above." Kohut's openness to such exceptional cases is encouraging, but to deal with such dreams he has to leave his usual assumptions about the formation of dreams and the appropriate method of dream analysis, i.e. discovering the latent dream through an examination of the dreamer's free associations.

In summary, the psychoanalytic perspective has not appreciably furthered dream interpretation in the psychology of religion even though we owe much to Freud and other psychoanalysts for their role in the general development of dream analysis. Freud's psychoanalytic approach reduces potentially religious symbols and motifs in dreams to Oedipal themes of sex and aggression or to even earlier stages of ego development. Psychoanalysis has proved valuable in carefully observing instinctual impulses, in calling attention to repression which frequently generates the symbols of these impulses in dreams, and in purging religion of some of its more regressive elements. While psychoanalysis has helped to chart the territory of the unconscious and has offered an account of the dynamics of the unconscious, it has not recognized the possibility of revelation in dreams. Although the major streams of psychoanalytic thought after Freud are generally more sympathetic to the roles of religion than Freud was, they have not extended their theory of dream interpretation to include an encounter with spiritual realities in dreams. While Kohut shows surprising openness to a few exceptional cases of "dreams from above," this does not represent an integral part of his theory about dreams.

Humanistic Psychology of Religion

The study of "normal" human beings and their development is a primary focus of humanistic psychology. In *Toward a Psychology of Being* Abraham Maslow contrasts this "psychology of being" with "deficiency psychology" or abnormal psychology. While Maslow himself does not rely on dreams to understand the psyche, his views and attitudes have shaped the theoretical context within which humanistic psychologists deal with dreams. Maslow helped humanistic psychology to take values and religious experience seriously, and to include "transcendence" as a legitimate concern for psychology. The underlying assumption of the Third Force, Maslow's term for humanistic psychology, is that there is an inner nature in the human being that is either morally neutral or positively good. In this view destructiveness, sadism, cruelty and other manifestations of evil are not intrinsic, but rather reactions against the frustration of inner needs. Since the inner nature of humans is good or at least neutral, the therapeutic goal of humanistic psychology is to bring out and encourage the person's inner nature rather than suppress it.

The term "peak experience" is one of the hallmarks of Maslow's psychology of being. He found that practically everyone has peak experiences but often they don't know it. The humanistic therapist or counselor helps people recognize these "small mystical experiences" when they occur.[57] Maslow studied peak experiences by asking groups and individuals questions such as "What was the most ecstatic moment of your life?" or "Have you ever experienced transcendent ecstasy?"[58] He found from the responses that the two most frequent ways to get peak experiences are through music and sex.

Maslow maintains that ego defense mechanisms are a major obstacle to having and recognizing peak experiences. He describes "desacralization" as a defense mechanism not dealt with in psychology textbooks. According to Maslow, people desacralize other people when they reduce them to objects and refuse to see their value in the "light of eternity." Self-actualization requires us to give up this ego-defense and learn to resacralize, i.e. be willing again to see the sacred, the symbolic and the eternal and to view people "under the aspect of eternity."[59] The therapist should be open to dealing with questions about religion and the meaning of life when they emerge in the consulting room.

When Maslow speaks in traditionally religious language to describe peak experiences as "small mystical experiences" and "transcendent ecstasy," we might ask how he, as a humanistic psychologist, understands transcendence. Maslow devoted a lengthy article to this subject and concluded with this condensed statement:

> "Transcendence refers to the very highest and most inclusive or holistic levels of human consciousness, behaving and relating, as ends rather than means, to oneself, to significant others, to human beings in general, to other species, to nature, and to the cosmos."[60]

Transcendence then refers beyond individual human consciousness and extends to the entire human species, to other species and the cosmos. At the outer limits, Maslow's description of transcendence sounds almost theological though he steps back from the religious potential of his definition:

> Transcendence also means to become divine or godlike, to go beyond the merely human. But one must be careful here not to make anything extrahuman or supernatural out of this kind of statement. I am thinking of using the word "metahuman" or "B-human" in order to stress that this becoming very high or divine or godlike is part of human nature even though it is not often seen in fact. It is still a potentiality of human nature.[61]

It is not entirely clear what a "non-supernatural" divinity might be like, or how the divine is "still a potentiality of human nature." In another definition of transcendence he also speaks in religious terms about the consequence of a "climactic peak-experience":

> After the insight or the great conversion, or the great mystic experience, or the great illumination, or the great full awakening, one can calm down as the novelty disappears and as one gets used to good things or even great things, live casually in heaven and be on easy terms with the eternal and the infinite.[62]

Again we see Maslow juxtapose the terms human and divine in an unusual way. He uses terms usually reserved for spiritual transformation to define human transcendence: "the great conversion," "the great mystic experience," "the great illumination." It is hard to tell whether he is expanding the definition of "human" or contracting the term "divine" when he speaks of living casually in heaven and of being on easy terms with the eternal and the infinite. Maslow insists he is referring to "the mystical experience as classically described by the religious mystics in the various religious literatures,"[63] but as these experiences are classically described they frequently imply a supernatural Other and not strictly human potential. Is he saying these mystics had the same experience he is discussing but their supernatural interpretation was mistaken? Or is he referring to the more pantheistic varieties of mystical experience, such as those described by Meister Eckhart or in Zen Buddhism? He never clarifies this point.

In yet another definition of transcendence he searches for a way to express the elusive character of the "divine" human potential:

> As a particular kind of transcendence useful for certain theoretical purposes is the transcendence of human limits, imperfections, shortcomings, and finiteness. This comes either in the acute end experiences of perfection or in the plateau experiences of perfection, in which one can *be* an end, a god, a perfection, an essence, a Being (rather

than a Becoming), sacred, divine. This can be phrased as a transcendence of ordinary, everyday humanness or metahumanness or some such phrasing. This can be an actual phenomenological state; it can be a kind of cognizing; it can also be a conceived limit of philosophy or ideal—for instance, the platonic essences or ideas . . . Perhaps the best word in order to stress that this is part of human nature even though at its best, is the word metahumanness.[64]

When he speaks of the "actual phenomenological state" it appears he implies a phenomenological method which suspends judgment on the metaphysical status of the experience. In his discussion of these transcendent states he uses what William James calls the language of "over-belief." He expresses personal beliefs about the essence of these experiences that go beyond detailed descriptions and seem to affirm belief in the spiritual and even supernatural reality of what is experienced or symbolized. At the same time he maintains he does not want these statements interpreted in supernatural terms. While Maslow does not reflect on methodology here, it would seem he is using traditional religious words as a phenomenological description.

Another key figure in the humanistic psychology of religion is Gordon Allport. As he points out in the introduction to his classic, *The Individual and His Religion*, his view is consistent with modern psychotherapy and neo-Freudianism.[65] Allport studies religion in the "normally mature and productive personality," he does not focus on the psychopathology of religion as Freud tended to do. He maintains that a person's attitudes and religious beliefs greatly determine his mental and physical health. He also notes that religion highlights the need for relationship and love in a way that is often lacking in psychotherapy.[66] Like William James he sees no single, unique religious emotion, but rather notices a widely divergent set of emotions and experiences that may be focused upon a variety of religious objects. Also, like James, he stressed the importance of emotion in religion, though where James spoke primarily of religious experience, Allport preferred to speak of the religious "sentiment." While Allport does not discuss dreams in his description of psychotherapy, he does express the general goals of integrating discordant impulses and aspirations and unifying the personality which are also characteristic of humanistic dream interpretation. He notes that both psychology and religion share these therapeutic goals.[67]

Allport sees the conflict between the impulsively desirable and the morally obligatory as a major cause of mental disturbances. Here he recognizes what Freud spoke of as super-ego and id conflicts and what humanistic psychologist Carl Rogers referred to as a conflict between organismic needs and conceived values. This conflict illustrates how religion and ethics can be sources of mental problems becuse they often restrict the body's impulses. Dreams frequently portray these conflicts in dramatic and concrete images of parents, police and judges versus drunks, letchers and killers. Allport does not refer his discussion of this conflict to dreams but his strategy of knitting together discordant personality elements is similar to working with a subjective dream interpretation.[68] Even though religion and ethics can be a source of inner division, they can also integrate the personality. According to Allport religion has great integrative power because its goals are never quite fulfilled and only unfinished tasks can integrate the psyche effectively.[69]

Allport describes the many factors that contribute to the religious sentiment in people, including bodily needs, temperament, spiritual interests and values, pursuit of rational explanations of experience and responses to the surrounding culture.[70] Allport observed that people increasingly agree with the humanistic proposition that religion should be "regarded entirely as a natural human function; it should have nothing whatever to do with supernatural notions."[71] Here Allport focuses on the fundamentally humanistic point that God is essentially a symbol of the highest human value and therefore it does not refer primarily to a transcendent deity. Were he to work with dreams, we can assume he would also interpret religious dream imagery according to this same humanistic principle so that religious images would symbolize aspects of the dreamer's own personality.

Yet another person who has shaped humanistic psychology of religion is Erich Fromm. Although he was trained as a psychoanalyst he is more frequently thought of as a humanistic psychotherapist and a neo-Freudian (a term he disliked). Fromm uses the term "humanistic" in a very appreciative sense and applies it to his understanding of religion. He says humanistic religion is the type of religion which develops human strength as opposed to authoritarian religion which alienates man from his own powers. According to Fromm this distinction cuts across theistic and non-theistic lines.[72] Authoritarian religion projects humanity's best onto God and thereby deprives it of these qualities. Fromm characterizes this form of religion as focusing on obedience, thus creating a mood of sorrow and guilt. He says that the surrender called for in authoritarian religion allows its members to lose their sense of aloneness and limitation, but they also lose their integrity and independence. He finds this attitude represented in Calvin's theology though not exclusively so.[73]

Fromm contrasts this authoritarian religion with humanistic religion where the prevailing mood is joy and faith is considered to be conviction based on experience rather than assent to doctrines. This form of religion encourages human reason to understand man and the world. The main virtue of humanistic religion is self-realization and the chief sin is trying to escape from human freedom and responsibility.[74] Fromm finds this humanistic type of religion in early Buddhism, Taoism, Isaiah, Jesus, Socrates and the mystics. Like Allport he points out that in theistic varieties of humanistic religion God is a symbol of man's own powers, not a force having power over man. According to the criteria of humanistic religion he maintains that Freud, the avowed atheist, was religious in the best sense of the word. He finds Freud's ideals of truth, freedom, independence, responsibility, and reducing suffering to be consistent with the ethical core of all the great religions.[75]

Compared with Freud's assessment of religion, Fromm appears very sympathetic. He judges religion by its fruits, much like William James did. If the effects contribute to growth, strength, freedom and happiness, then that religion is valuable;

if they constrict human potential, curtail productivity and reduce happiness, that religion is destructive.[76] Fromm values only certain aspects of religion such as the sense of wonder and ultimate concern, ritual as shared action expressing common devotion to ideals and dogma as a symbolic language expressing the depths of human experience. Fromm criticizes the quasi-scientific claims of religion (e.g. using the Bible to explain the natural world), the magical manipulation of nature and irrational rituals used to fend off guilt due to unconscious destructive impulses.[77]

Fromm's understanding of dreams is somewhere between that of Freud and Jung. He recognizes with Freud that dreams may express irrational and asocial strivings and with Jung that dreams reveal unconscious wisdom transcending the individual.[78] He holds the view that dreams express all kinds of mental activity, both the lowest and the highest. Of course Jung was also aware of the value of a Freudian interpretation of dreams, since he followed that model until his researches into schizophrenics' visionary imagery and the psychology of religion led him to hypothesize the collective, transpersonal activity of the psyche. So Fromm's dream interpretation approximates Jung's in so far as he recognizes the potential wisdom of the unconscious, but he differs sharply with Jung on the source of the dream's intelligence and purposiveness. Where Jung sees a transcending source, Fromm prefers to see a source that does not transcend the individual's own intellectual and moral capacity:

> The difference between Jung's interpretation and my own can be summed up in this statement. There is agreement that we often are wiser and more decent in our sleep than in our waking life. Jung explains this phenomenon with the assumption of a source of revelation transcending us, while I believe that what we think in our sleep is *our* thinking . . .[79]

Earlier, when considering Maslow's work, we saw the complexity of the transcendence concept. Humanists favor those definitions of transcendence which retain their connection to human powers and potential and this also applies to Fromm's position.

Fromm's approach to religious elements in dreams can be seen in his reinterpretation of two dreams Jung presented in *Psychology and Religion*. Both Jung's and Fromm's interpretation are interesting in that they show how the theories of an analyst influence dream interpretation. The dream is that of a non-practicing Catholic. I shall present just enough of the dream to make sense of Fromm's interpretation.

> There are many houses which have a theatrical character, a sort of stage scenery . . . One of the houses is distinguished by a signboard with the following inscription:
>
> > This is the universal Catholic church
> > It is the church of the Lord
> > All those who feel themselves to be
> > instruments of the Lord may enter.
>
> And below in smaller letters:
>
> > The church is founded by Jesus and Paul
>
> —it is as if a firm boasted of its old standing. I say to my friend, "Let us go in and have a look." He replies, "I do not see why many people should be together in order to have religious feelings." But I say "You are a Protestant, so you will never understand it. There is a woman nodding approval . . .
>
> We now enter the church. The interior resembles a mosque rather than a church, as a matter of fact it is particularly like the Hagia Sophia. There are no chairs, which produces a wonderful effect of space. There are also no images. There are only framed sentences on the walls (like those in the Hagia Sophia). One of these sentences reads, "Do not flatter your benefactor." The same woman who nodded approval to me before begins to weep and says, "I think that it is perfectly all right," but she vanishes.
>
> . . . people in front of me . . . pronounce the following words: "we confess that we are under the power of the Lord. The Kingdom of Heaven is within ourselves." They repeat this thrice in a most solemn way. Then the organ plays a fugue by Bach and a choir sings. Sometimes it is

music alone, sometimes the following words are repeated: "Everything else is paper," which means that it does not produce a living impression.

When the music is finished the second part of the ceremony begins, as is the custom at students' meetings where the dealing with serious affairs is followed by the gay part of the gathering . . . A priest explains to me: "These somewhat futile amusements are officially acknowledged and admitted. We must adapt a little to American methods. If you have to deal with big crowds, as we have, it is inevitable. We differ, however, on principle from the American churches in that we cherish an emphatically anti-ascetic tendency." Whereupon I woke up with a feeling of great relief.[80]

Jung interpreted this dream as a dramatic representation of the dreamer's compromise between Catholicism and pagan *joie de vivre*. Fromm disagrees:

The dreamer is indeed concerned with religion but not, as Jung assumes, arriving at a flat compromise but at a very clear concept of the difference between authoritarian and humanistic religion. Authoritarian religion, a system in which obedience is the basic virtue and man makes himself small and powerless, giving all power and strength to God, is the type of religion he fights against; this battle is the same which pervades his personal life, the rebellion against any kind of authoritarian domination. What he is striving for is humanistic religion, where the emphasis is on man's strength and goodness and where virtue is not obedience but the realization of one's human powers.[81]

The contrasting styles of religion described in the dream do roughly correspond to Fromm's two basic types of religion but when he sees in the dream a "bitter accusation against religion" he stretches the manifest dream to fit his own attitude. There is much more ambivalence in this dream than Fromm allows. The female figure (perhaps a mother figure, as Fromm suggests, or an anima figure, as Jung supposes) seems to approve the dreamer's willingness to investigate and maybe even appreciate some of the elements connected with institutional religion. The woman also weeps and then leaves after the dreamer reads the inscription "Do not flatter your benefactor," indicating that she is not at home in such stark, anti-traditional forms of religion. So the "bitter accusation" against "authoritarian religion" is mostly Fromm's own, just as he expresses this same opinion throughout *Psychoanalysis and Religion.*

Fromm's reinterpretation of another dream of the same patient illustrates his reluctance to interpret religious dream symbols in a transcendent direction. Here is the dream:

> I am entering a solemn house. It is called "the house of inner composure or self collection." In the background are many burning candles arranged so as to form four pyramid-like points. An old man stands at the door of the house. People enter, they do not talk and often stand still in order to concentrate. The old man at the door tells me about the visitors to the house and says: "When they leave they are pure." I enter the house now, and I am able to concentrate completely. A voice says: "What thou art doing is dangerous. Religion is not a tax which thou payest in order to get rid of the woman's image for this image is indispensable. Woe to those who use religion as a substitute for the other side of the soul's life. They are in error and they shall be cursed. Religion is no substitute, but it is the ultimate accomplishment added to every other activity of the soul. Out of the fullness of life thou shalt give birth to thy religion and only then shalt thou be blessed." Together with the last sentence a faint music becomes audible, simple tunes played by an organ, reminding me somewhat of Wagner's "Fire magic" (Feuerzauber). As I leave the house I have the vision of a flaming mountain and I feel that a fire which can not be quenched must be a sacred fire.[82]

Again Fromm relates this dream to his distinction between humanistic and authoritarian religion. He interprets the woman's image to mean love and sex and finds Jung's interpretation of her as the anima or a personification of the unconscious to be "one-sided and dogmatic."[83] The interpretations of Jung and Fromm are not significantly different, however, when we realize that often a man's unconscious (woman as symbol of dreamer's unconscious) links him to his feelings and sexual life (woman as symbol of love and sex). The message is essentially the same—religion is not a substitute for contact with human feelings, sexuality and the unconscious.

Another important symbol in this dream which Fromm and Jung interpret differently is the sacred fire. Jung sees the unquenchable fire as a symbol of God while Fromm views it as a symbol of love and sex. We would have to know more about the dreamer's own associations before deciding which interpretation is more fitting. In the dream context both interpretations make sense as goals of the dreamer's development. Fromm might add, as a humanist, that fire as a God symbol is really speaking about the depths of human love anyway.

We have seen that Maslow incorporated the language of transcendence into his work in such a way that he became involved in a transpersonal interpretation of human potential. When we look at other developments in humanistic psychology, such as Gestalt dream work, we also discover an openness to transcendence. Fritz Perls' own approach to religious dream images, including images of God, would be to interpret them as projected aspects of the dreamers' personality. Perls would be concerned with whether the dream images of God or the gods were integrated with other aspects of the personality. To become aware of and integrate the religious images (and whatever psychological characteristics they represent) with their polar opposites would be Perls' strategy. For example, if the dream image of God is considered to represent a dominating aspect of the dreamer's personality, the Gestaltist would explore this in relation to its polar opposite, the submissive or inferior personality characteristics.

Beyond Perls work with the dream as projection of the dreamer's personality, there have been important developments in Gestalt theory in the last decade which have a direct bearing on dream interpretation in the psychology of religion. Jorge Rosner, who has co-founded a network of Gestalt training institutes in Canada, the United States, Denmark, Sweden and

Australia, has advanced the theory and practice of Gestalt therapy by emphasizing the spiritual dimensions of psychotherapy and personal growth.[84] Rosner views Gestalt not simply as a form of psychotherapy but as a way of life. In dream interpretation he considers the possibility that dreams open onto other worlds. In his work with dreams he also recognizes transpersonal phenomena such as telepathy, precognition, clairvoyance and religious experience. Rosner's explorations have pushed Gestalt therapy beyond the limits of humanistic psychology into the territory of transpersonal psychology.

Rosnerian Gestalt contributes to a non-reductive interpretation of dreams. While affirming many of the clinical observations in psychoanalysis and humanistic psychology, Rosner goes beyond an instinctual and personal interpretation of dream symbols to include a transpersonal interpretation. The most important guide to interpreting these transpersonal forces is the meaning they have for the dreamer. As with the schools of transpersonal psychology, Rosnerian Gestalt relies upon the phenomenological method where the question about the truth or falsity of an experience is suspended and describing the experience in great detail becomes central. Thus in a dream where Jesus, the Buddha, or spirits of the dead appear, the dreamer may be thought to actually encounter them in an altered state of consciousness. This hypothesis undergirds not only the experience of spiritual phenomena but also psychic phenomena such as telepathy, precognition or clairvoyance.

Humanistic psychology has given aspects of religion a central place in its thought and practice. Its analysis of the transcendent potential of human beings opens the way to the possibility of an explicitly religious interpretation of dreams. Since the dreamer is largely responsible for the ultimate meaning discovered in his or her dreams, the dreamer's own world view and religious beliefs determine the accent of reality given to religious and spiritual symbols in dreams. Dreamers may testify that they encountered God on the basis of their personal beliefs and the uncanny power of some religious symbols. Many humanistic psychologists may have their own reservations about such interpretations, nevertheless, humanists like Maslow, recognize that the farther reaches of human nature are not so clearly defined that we know for certain whether or not religious symbols actually open onto the spiritual world and the divine.

Transpersonal Psychology of Religion

In chapter two I discussed the primary concerns of transpersonal psychology. Where humanistic psychology views personality functioning in terms of the awareness, identity, conflicts, values, attitudes and world view of the conscious psyche, transpersonal psychology seeks to understand the influence of forces, symbols and realities which originate beyond the individual's psyche.[85] Although transpersonal psychology did, in a sense, grow out of humanistic psychology, its concern with "transcendent" influences connect it back to Plato, St. Augustine, William James, Carl Jung and Eastern religious disciplines.[86] Carl Jung and his followers recognize the value of dream interpretation in studying transpersonal phenomena. Of course, not all Jungian analysts emphasize the explicitly religious interpretation of dreams. For instance, James Hall writes in *Jungian Analysis*:

> We no longer tend to think of the human world as existing within an encompassing divine order, whose ordination of future human destiny can at times be seen in revelatory dreams. In the modern world since Freud, dreams have lost the role of messenger between gods and humanity and have become messages between the ego and the unconscious, if indeed they are not reduced to the function of disguising unacceptable thoughts in order to preserve sleep.

Some dreams are messages between the ego and the unconscious but that does not rule out the possibility that other dreams may reveal dimensions of the spirit world or the divine. Hall describes a very productive hypothesis for Jungian dream interpretation in the clinical setting, nevertheless, this still remains only one of many hypotheses and not necessarily the only productive or "correct" one.[87]

John Dourley, a Roman Catholic priest and Jungian analyst, emphasizes the revelatory potential of dreams in his discussion of Jung's attitude toward Christianity. He praises Jung's Gnostic-Christian perspective on dreams as a means of personal revelation:

> Instead of considering revelation to be somehow over and done with, ending with the historical closing of the canon, a psychological perspective would understand revelation to continue in the individual dialogue between ego and unconscious. The New Testament or Covenant would cease to be a once-upon-a-time contract whose terms are spelled out in sacred texts. Rather a genuinely *new* testament would be struck every time the individual was led by the Self into dialogue with it, in the interest of its (the Self's) more conscious incarnation.[88]

Dourley feels that guidance provided by the Self archetype is more personally suited to Christians than universal spiritual directives or undifferentiated moral advice given by the church.[89]

Jung's own position on the meaning of God and the spiritual world changed radically over his long career. James Heisig traces three distinct stages in the development of Jung's position.[90] In the first stage (c. 1900-1921), Jung tended to reduce religious experience to the projection of emotional states. As with projections in general, what is actually within the individual's own mind is experienced as originating in the environment. This is similar to Freud's position in that it reduces an apparent experience of the divine to the personal dynamics of the individual's psyche.

The second stage of Jung's thought (c. 1921-1945) reflects his theory of the archetypes. Here religious experiences are viewed as projections from the deep layers of the psyche. In this case the materials that are projected are products of the patterns of imagination and perception Jung calls the archetypes.[91] In this case he considers religious experience a result of transpersonal dynamics, that is, factors that are not due to personal experiences in the individual's life, yet he does not relate the religious experience to an external and transcendent reality.

The third stage of Jung's thought (c. 1945-1961) is not so clearly reductionistic as the first two stages. In this period there is evidence that Jung suspended judgment on the relationship of archetypal patterns of imagination to the spiritual entities they may symbolize. This attitude of suspended judgment appears to be akin to William James' attitude toward religious phenomena and reflects Jung's application of the phenomenological method. According to this approach an observer would not attempt to judge what the essence of a religious experience might be, but would try to determine what the experience means to the person who has it. This method allows experiences to speak for themselves and avoids imposing theoretical categories and expectations onto religious experience. This open attitude to religious phenomena is partly what Jung was trying to get at with his notion of psychological truth. For Jung psychological truth refers to the fact that an idea such as God has existed for a long time and in the minds of many. This does not mean that the reality reference of the idea is correct in an objective sense but only that the idea has had a certain psychological existence and value.

While Jung's way of expressing the importance of universal ideas or themes such as God or the spirit world is problematic, it has the merit of taking these ideas seriously rather than dismissing them as wishes, emotions, or illusions. Increasingly Jung became aware of the limitation of what he could say about spiritual phenomena as a clinician and scientist. As a clinician he recognized the importance of religious ideas and symbols in the functioning of his patient's psyche whether or not these ideas were true in the sense of their corresponding to realities in the world beyond that person. As a scientist he realized that there was no way to determine in any final sense whether religious ideas correspond to the actual realities symbolized. To talk about the truth or falsity of religious ideas would be, for Jung, to enter the realm of metaphysics which is not subject to the same empirical verification as science.

In some of his later writings Jung formulated this relationship between the subjective experience of God or the God-image and the objective realities symbolized in the experience:

It is only through the psyche that we can establish that God acts upon us, but we are unable to distinguish whether these actions emanate from God or from the unconscious. We cannot tell whether God and the unconscious are two different entities. Both are border-line concepts for transcendental contents. But empirically it can be established, with a sufficient degree of probability, that there is in the unconscious an archetype of wholeness which manifests itself spontaneously in dreams, etc., and a tendency independent of the conscious will, to relate other archetypes to this center. Consequently, it does not seem improbable that the archetype of wholeness occupies as such a central position which approximates it to the God-image. The similarity is further borne out by the peculiar fact that the archetype produces a symbolism which has always characterized and expressed the Deity. These facts make possible a certain qualification of our above thesis concerning the indistinguishableness of God and the unconscious. Strictly speaking, the God-image does not coincide with the unconscious as such, but with a special content of it, namely the archetype of the self. It is this archetype from which we can no longer distinguish the God-image empirically.[92]

Jung was even more explicit regarding the possibility of God's influence on the human psyche in the following passages:

We are so captivated by and entangled in our subjective consciousness that we have simply forgotten the age-old fact that God speaks chiefly through dreams and visions.[93]

In spite of the fact that the Catholic Church admits the occurrence of dreams sent by God, most of its thinkers make no attempt to understand them. I also doubt whether there is a Protestant treatise on dogmatics that would "stoop so low" as to consider the possibility that the *vox Dei* might be perceived in a dream. But if somebody really believes in God, by what authority does he suggest that God is unable to speak through dreams?[94]

In these statements we see that Jung is at least open to the possibility that the individual may be in direct contact with transcendent realities through the medium of dreams. It appears that for Jung transpersonal dimensions of experience can go beyond collective aspects of human nature to include contact with and influence by transcendent realities.

Although an effective clinical interpretation might see the dream figures of Jesus and the Buddha as symbols of the dreamer's own spiritual center, the objective reality reference of these dream images cannot simply be ruled out. In dreams dealing with the spirit world or the divine realm, the meaning of the dream may not only be referring to aspects of ourselves, or to our unconscious attitude toward the spirits or God, but we may also be encountering those spiritual realities directly. In Jung's own dreams involving the dead, he went beyond interpretation on the subjective level, demonstrating his openness to religious phenomena in dreams.

Another important figure in transpersonal psychology is Roberto Assagioli. His "psychosynthesis" is a good example of transpersonal psychology's interest in religion and spiritual interpretations of unconscious processes. According to Assagioli, psychosynthesis is concerned with two kinds of growth in awareness: 1) the awakening and development of latent potentialities (like Maslow's self-actualization) and 2) the experience and awareness of a "synthesizing spiritual Center."[95] As a psychotherapy psychosynthesis aims to reconstruct the personality around the new center.

In Assagioli's view of the mind, the higher unconscious or superconscious is the source of higher intuitions, urges to humanitarian and heroic action, altruistic love and states of contemplation, illumination and ecstasy.[96] He says that in some universal geniuses the normal personality center penetrates to the superconscious level and thereby achieves a more or less permanent self-realization. In other exceptional people, elements from the superconscious descend into the normal field of consciousness.[97] In spiritual psychosynthesis the spiritual Self pervades the renewed personality. He also speaks of this self-realization process as a more or less temporary identification or blending of ego consciousness with the spiritual Self. Assagioli explains that there are not two selves, but rather the personal self (ego consciousness) is a reflection of the spiritual Self. When asked what the nature of this transpersonal Self is like, he said:

> I cannot tell you what the transpersonal self is like. Maslow tried to characterize it and the nature of the peak experience in *The Psychology of Being*. Direct experience of the transpersonal self is rare and union with it is very rare. But many people have a knowledge of it that is mediated through the higher unconsciousness or the super-consciousness. I can describe some of the effects. It is spontaneously manifested in the creative works of the great universal geniuses such as Plato, Dante, and Einstein. Others get in touch with it through prayer or meditation. Or they may feel a call or pull from some Higher Power. Language is always inadequate to speak about transpersonal or spiritual experiences. Every expression is highly symbolic, and a large variety of symbols have been used: enlightenment, descent into the underworld of the psyche, awakening, purification, transmutation, psychospiritual alchemy, rebirth, and liberation.[98]

Although contact with the spiritual Self may produce dramatic effects in creative works of genius or in spiritual experiences, in other cases this contact does not produce creative or mystical experience.

Assagioli holds that elements and states emerging from the superconscious, such as spiritual inspirations, mystical consciousness and religious experiences are factual and real in the pragmatic sense because they produce changes in the inner and outer world.[99] For Assagioli this means these spiritual phenomena are open to observation and scientific experiment. As a scientist he is aware of the limits of his statements on religious symbols and experiences. As he puts it, "psychosynthesis does not aim or attempt to give a metaphysical nor a theological explanation of the great Mystery—it leads to the door, but it stops there."[100] He is open to various philosophies so long as they don't deny the existence of spiritual realities.

Assagioli adopts a phenomenological position that takes seriously reports of direct experience of spiritual realities given by founders of religion, mystics, some philosophers, and many other people.[101] In fact he says one purpose of spiritual psychosynthesis is to help to attain direct spiritual experience but he adds that mystical experiences are not goals in themselves.[102] These experiences provide enthusiasm and incentive to serve man and God and are valued to the degree they contribute to increased creativity and the ability to give yourself to someone or some field of work.

Assagioli recommends a number of techniques to promote contact with a person's spiritual center. Dream interpretation is only one of the many techniques he uses to explore the unconscious and spiritual potential. Generally Assagioli prefers meditation, initiated symbol projection and inner dialogue because they are faster and more systematic than dream interpretation since they do not rely completely on what emerges of its own accord from the unconscious.

For meditation exercises he draws upon the work of Carl Happich who combined his experience of modern depth psychology with Oriental meditation techniques. Happich's "meditative psychotherapy" emphasizes the importance of breathing in opening meditation to deeper affective states. He uses breathing exercises before therapy sessions to develop increased passivity of respiration and then introduces a series of meditations designed to evoke archetypal symbols that bring deeper self-knowledge.[103] Three major symbols he uses are meadow, mountain and chapel. He interprets the meadow as a symbol of the child's world, the active and creative "child" within the client. A healthy person will often experience a meadow with children, a mate, flowers and lush foliage. The psychically ill person often visualizes the meadow as wilted and maybe only a few stumps for trees. Happich assumes that the meadow visualized is a symbolic representation of the person's psychic condition.

In the mountain meditation a person will frequently symbolize some obstacle in the way as a challenge to overcome. Passing through the forest on the way up the mountain is an occasion for coming to terms with the dark and fearful side of life and nature. For Happich the movement described during the climb represents the client's capacity to develop toward psychic freedom.[104] The chapel meditation is the most explicitly religious symbol Happich uses. It brings the client in touch with his or her attitude toward the central problems of human life and the possibility of psychic transformation.

Another technique Assagioli employs is Initiated Symbol Projection, a psycho-diagnostic and psycho-therapeutic technique developed in West Germany since 1948.[105] He uses a standard set of twelve symbols to examine the client's psyche. Beyond this work, he uses two other groups of symbols to evoke the spiritual Self: 1) geometrical and nature symbols and 2) person symbols. Among his geometrical symbols are the sun, stars and a sphere of fire; the rose and lotus are two of the most important nature symbols he selects. According to Assagioli these symbols may initiate or illustrate the process towards and the achievement of spiritual psychosynthesis and person symbols such as the Angel, the Inner Christ, the Inner Warrior, the Old Sage, and the Inner Teacher usually establish a relationship between the personal self and the spiritual Self.[106]

He also uses the Inner Dialogue Technique to work with the person symbols. He asks the client to imagine he has a specific problem to bring to his Inner Teacher and to talk to his imagined teacher realistically as if he were a living person and then to await a response. This technique is much like Gestalt dreamwork or Jungian active imagination where the client carries on a dialogue between dream figures and between the dreamer and a dream figure.

While Assagioli discusses symbols and their interpretation primarily in terms of meditation, initiated symbol projection and inner dialogue, he applies the same principles of interpretation in his analysis of dreams.[107] The symbols and situations used in these techniques also emerge spontaneously in dreams, and Assagioli considers a spiritual interpretation of them. As a psychologist he does not judge the ontological status of these symbols as they appear in dreams, but rather he follows very carefully the description of the client. He does not reveal whether he believes that the Inner Christ relates to a transcendent reality outside the dreamer. He employs the language of divine immanence, but we cannot be certain of his attitude toward divine transcendence. And just as with Maslow and Jung we cannot be sure if he believes that human transcendence is the same as divine immanence. These questions take us into the territory of personal religious beliefs about the realities symbolized in psychic life.

We cannot solve these problems completely in a theoretical way but must return to the meaning religious symbols have for individual dreamers. The most we can conclude from this discussion of dream interpretation in the psychology of religion is that certain representatives of each force of psychology have been open to some spiritual dimensions of dream interpretation. These psychologists recognize the limits of our present knowledge about dream symbols and they have helped to establish the theoretical framework within which we practice dream interpretation in the psychology of religion. Now we turn to specific rules of dream interpretation which take into account the theoretical foundation described in this chapter.

Notes

1. While there are many approaches within the psychology of religion, most of them have nothing to do with the study of dreams. For readers who would like a summary of the methods, general history and development of the psychology of religion there have been a number of valuable works in this area over the last fifteen years providing a comprehensive view of the discipline. Among the best studies are O. Strunk, ed., *The Psychology of Religion: Historical and Interpretive Readings* (1971; this includes some of the earlier reviews of literature in the field); W. Oates, *The Psychology of Religion* (1973; a good discussion of the phenomenological and developmental perspectives in the psychology of religion); L.B. Brown, *Psychology and Religion* (1973; includes behavioral studies from the *Journal for the Scientific Study of Religion*); M. Argyle and B. Beit-Hallahmi, *The Social Psychology of Religion* (1975; describes trends in the discipline, summarizes studies correlating religion with age, sex differences, and social class); H. Faber, *Psychology of Religion* (1976; reviews the major perspectives of depth psychology on religion); N. Malony, *Current Perspectives in the Psychology of Religion* (1977; a comprehensive survey of what has been happening in the psychology of religion since the late 19th century; it situates the contribu-

tions of William James, Stanley Hall, Edwin Starbuck, James Pratt and others in the early days of the discipline; also contains a useful summary of information sources and methods of investigation in the field); J. Tisdale, *Growing Edges in the Psychology of Religion* (1980; a good selection of readings, including bilateral asymmetry studies in brain research); C.D. Batson and W. L. Ventis, *The Religious Experience: A Social Psychological Perspective* (1982; an excellent discussion of scientific methods in this discipline and a review of empirical research on religion and age, sex, race, socio-economic status, education and mental health); B. Spilka, R. Hood and R. Gorsuch, *The Psychology of Religion: An Empirical Approach* (1985: reviews empirical research on religious development, religious experience, and religion and behavior): and L.B. Brown, ed., *Advances in the Psychology of Religion* (1985; illuminating articles discussing current trends, methods and results of recent research).

The setting for research in the psychology of religion determines to a certain extent whether experimental, psychoanalytic, humanistic, transpersonal, historical, clinical or other methods will be used. In some colleges and universities, the discipline is conducted in the psychology department (e.g. Wheaton College, Massachusetts or the University of Kansas) and there the experimental method predominates, whereas in other places it occurs in the department of religious studies (e.g. the University of Toronto) and there the perspectives of depth psychology are currently primary.

2. Walter Houston Clark, a major figure in the contemporary psychology of religion, has called James' *Varieties* ". . . the most notable of all books in the field of psychology of religion and probably destined to be the most influential book written on religion in the 20th century." N. Malony, *Current Perspectives in the Psychology of Religion* (Grand Rapids, 1977), p. 228.

3. *The Varieties of Religious Experience*, p. 42.

4. Depth psychology refers to those psychological approaches which employ the concept of the unconscious to understand human experience and behavior.

5. James' own case of melancholia and panic fear is well disguised as the translation of a report originally given in French. *Varieties*, pp. 135-136. James himself thought that his experience had a "religious bearing."

6. *Ibid.*, pp. 62-64, 71.

7. *Ibid.*, p. 64.

8. *Ibid.*, p. 38.

9. *Ibid.*, pp. 24, 29-34.

10. *Ibid.*, p. 64.

11. *Ibid.*, pp. 8, 238-244.

12. *Ibid.*, p. 34.

13. This article appeared in *Journal of Philosophy, Psychology and Scien-*

tific Methods, 7:85-92, 1910. Erik Erikson states that this was probably James' last publicly reported dream even though it was dreamed in 1906, four years before his death. See Erikson, *Identity, Youth and Crisis* (New York, 1968), p. 204.

14. "A Suggestion About Mysticism," p. 88.
15. *Ibid.*, pp. 88-89. The italics are in the original text.
16. *Varieties*, pp. 160-162.
17. *Ibid.*, pp. 140-156.
18. *The Principles of Psychology*, Vol. II (Cambridge, Mass., 1981), pp. 918-922.
19. *Varieties*, pp. 385-390.
20. *Ibid.*, pp. 135 and 298.
21. *Ibid.*, p. 90.
22. *Ibid.*, p. 90.
23. *Ibid.*, p. 92.
24. For example, Arthur Deikman's study on experimental meditation had eight subjects meditate on a vase and report their experience (*Altered States of Consciousness*, pp. 203-223). He concluded from the responses to this meditation procedure that meditation produces mystical experience and that many mystical phenomena partially deautomatize perception. In another study of meditation, Edward Maupin correlated personality factors with responses to a Zen meditation exercise (pp. 191-202). From this he concluded that tolerance for unrealistic experience and capacity for adaptive regression help to determine success in Zen meditation. An electroencephalographic study of meditation by Akira Kasamatsu and Tomio Hirai was able to show that there is a distinctive pattern of brain activity that is unlike hypnosis or sleep. These results confirm the view that Zen meditation is not simply a trance or dream state (pp. 501-514.

    The interesting feature of the first two experiments mentioned is their effort to combine phenomenological description with some attempt to isolate variables and quantify results. However, it is doubtful that these experiments actually confirm their hypotheses and demonstrate their conclusions since the experimental design is problematic. The short length of time in Deikman's and Maupin's studies are not sufficient to show anything reliable about the nature of meditation. Even the physiological study has drawbacks. It shows that Zen monks with 20 to 40 years of Zazen experience have a unique pattern of brain activity while meditating but it does not tell us much about their inner experience during or after meditation. These are just a couple of the problems with the experimental approach to psychology of religion, at least in the studies undertaken so far.

25. *Lucid Dreaming* (New York, 1986), p. 251.
26. *Ibid.*, pp. 262-264.
27. *Ibid.*, p. 263.
28. *Ibid.*, p. 264.

29. *Ibid.*, p. 268.
30. *Ibid.*, p. 269.
31. Hall, *The Meaning of Dreams* (New York, 1966), p. 85.
32. Rainey, *Freud as Student of Religion* (Missoula, Montana, 1975), pp. 36-47.
33. *Ibid.*, pp. 51-52.
34. *Totem and Taboo, SE* XIII, pp. 26-74. In an earlier work, "Obsessive Actions and Religious Practices" (1908) Freud speaks of religion as a "universal obsessional neurosis" (*SE* IX, pp. 126-127).
35. Freud's analysis in *Totem and Taboo* was based on Darwin's hypothesis that primitive man lived in hordes under the domination of a single powerful, jealous male. Freud assumed that the powerful father seized the women for himself and drove away or killed the sons. He further conjectured that the sons gathered together to kill the father and then regretted this deed. He sees their guilt as the origin of religion. *SE* XIII, pp. 125-126.
36. *The Future of an Illusion, SE* XXI, pp. 30-33.
37. *Civilization and Its Discontents, SE* XXI, p. 72.
38. Freud also discusses his view of religion in "Obsessional Actions and Religious Practices," (*SE* IX, pp. 115-127), *Group Psychology and the Analysis of the Ego* (*SE* XVIII, pp. 67-143), "Weltanschauung" in *New Introductory Lectures on Psychoanalysis* (*SE* XXII, pp. 158-182), "A Religious Experience" (*SE* XXI, pp. 169-172), and *Moses and Monotheism* (*SE* XXIII, pp. 3-137).
39. These three streams of psychoanalytic theory were used at the international psychoanalytic symposium at Delphi, Greece, in 1984, to give an overview of the general lines of psychoanalytic research after Freud.
40. H. Ruitenbeek (ed.), *Heirs to Freud* (Brattleboro, Vermont, 1967), p. 222.
41. The other major post-Freudian psychoanalytic contributor to the psychology of religion is Erich Fromm, but he will be considered later in the humanistic psychology of religion since he is more closely associated with that movement.
42. *Young Man Luther* (New York, 1962), p. 19.
43. "The Dream Specimen in Psychoanalysis," p. 21.
44. *Identity, Youth and Crisis* (New York, 1968), pp. 196-207 and *Childhood and Society* (New York, 1978), pp. 149-155.
45. *Childhood and Society*, pp. 149-155.
46. *Identity, Youth and Crisis*, pp. 197-207.
47. H. Fingarette, *The Self in Transformation* (New York, 1963), p. 196.
48. The American version of this movement is called interpersonal-relations theory and is represented by the work of Karen Horney, Erich Fromm and Harry Stack Sullivan. They emphasized the social factors in personality functioning to offset Freud's concentration on biological factors.

49. O. Kernberg, *Object Relations Theory and Clinical Psychoanalysis* (New York, 1976), p. 56.
50. H. Guntrip, *Psychoanalytic Theory, Therapy and the Self* (New York, 1973), pp. 191-194.
51. *Ibid.*, p. 8.
52. H. Kohut, *The Nature of the Psychoanalytic Cure* (Chicago, 1984), p. 76.
53. H. Kohut, *Self Psychology and the Humanities* (New York, 1985), pp. 7 and 14.
54. H. Kohut, *The Restoration of the Self* (New York, 1977), p. 46.
55. *Ibid.*, pp. 108-109.
56. H. Kohut, *Self Psychology and the Humanities*, p. 21.
57. A. Maslow, The Farther Reaches of Human Nature (New York, 1971), p. 47.
58. *Ibid.*, p. 168.
59. *Ibid.*, p. 48.
60. *Ibid.*, p. 269.
61. *Ibid.*, p. 264.
62. *Ibid.*, p. 265.
63. *Ibid.*, p. 261.
64. *Ibid.*, pp. 267-68.
65. Neo-Freudianism is the general approach represented by Erich Fromm, Karen Horney and Harry Stack Sullivan, which emphasizes present over past experience, and social over biological factors in personality functioning.
66. G. Allport, *The Individual and His Religion* (New York, 1960), p. 82.
67. *Ibid.*, pp. 77-79.
68. *Ibid.*, pp. 80-86.
69. *Ibid.*, p. 93.
70. *Ibid.*, pp. 8-9.
71. *Ibid.*, p. 43.
72. *Psychoanalysis and Religion* (New Haven, 1950), p. 35.
73. *Ibid.*, p. 34.
74. *Ibid.*, pp. 36-37.
75. *Ibid.*, p. 13.
76. *Ibid.*, p. 62.
77. *Ibid.*, pp. 97-107.
78. *The Forgotten Language* (New York, 1957), p. 109.
79. *Ibid.*, p. 97. Italics are in original text.
80. This dream text is originally found in C.G. Jung's *Psychology and Religion*, (*CW* 11, pp. 24-26) but I have used Erich Fromm's translation in *The Forgotten Language*, pp. 97-100.
81. E. Fromm, *The Forgotten Language*, p. 105.
82. Again the text is quoted from *The Forgotten Language*, pp. 106-107.
83. E. Fromm, *The Forgotten Language*, p. 107.

84. I. Starak discusses the basic principles of Rosnerian Gestalt in a paper presented at the Fifth Australian Conference on Family Psychotherapy in Canberra (5-8 September 1984). This unpublished paper, "Rosnerian Gestalt: Reconceptualizing Gestalt Therapy," describes Rosner's innovative methodology. I. Starak, T. Key and J. Oldham also describe Rosner's approach in *Risking Being Alive* (Victoria, Australia, 1978).

85. Ken Wilber, a major figure in contemporary transpersonal psychology of religion, explains the development of transpersonal psychology out of humanistic psychology this way: "The term 'transpersonal' was chosen to encompass those experiences and states in which the sense of awareness and identity apparently went beyond (trans) traditional personality and ego." *A Sociable God* (New York, 1983), p. ix.

86. The Oriental approaches to transpersonal phenomena provide detailed descriptions of "transcendent" states and technologies for attaining them at will. *Ibid.*, p. ix.

87. I shall discuss the need to recognize multiple hypotheses for dream interpretation in the psychology of religion in "Rules for Interpreting Dreams."

88. J. Dourley, *The Illness That We Are: A Jungian Critique of Christianity* (Toronto, 1984), p. 96.

89. *Ibid.*, p. 97. While Father Dourley speaks of the divine addressing individuals from their personal depths, he also argues for a strictly immanent interpretation of Jung's concept of the Self archetype. He says that the Self which is the source of dreams is the God within and he views a transcendent interpretation of the Self archetype as detracting from human responsibility and active participation in the divine drama.

90. J. Heisig, *Imago Dei: Jung's Psychology of Religion* (Lewisburg, Pa., 1979), pp. 31-43.

91. 'The archetype is . . . an inherited *tendency* of the human mind to form representations of mythological motifs—representations that vary a great deal without losing their basic pattern . . . They (archetypes) cannot be assigned to any particular time or religion or race. They are without known origin, and they can reproduce themselves even where transmission through migration must be ruled out." "Symbols and the Interpretation of Dreams," *CW* 18, p. 228.

92. Jung, *Answer to Job, CW* 11, pp. 468-69.

93. Jung, "Symbols and the Interpretation of Dreams," *CW* 18, p. 262.

94. *Ibid.*, p. 263.

95. *Psychosynthesis* (New York, 1965), p. 37.

96. *Ibid.*, pp. 17-18.

97. *Ibid.*, pp. 200-201.

98. In S. Keen, *Visions and Voices* (New York, 1970), p. 215.

99. *Psychosynthesis*, p. 6.

100. *Ibid.*, pp. 6-7.

101. *Ibid.*, p. 194.

102. *Ibid.*, pp. 195, 207.
103. *Ibid.*, pp. 305-306.
104. *Ibid.*, p. 308.
105. *Ibid.*, p. 287.
106. *Ibid.*, p. 203.
107. *Ibid.*, p. 304.

Dream Illustration No. 2

"Mandala Aflame"

I am walking at night in a thick fog. I can only see a few steps in front of me. Suddenly I notice something bright straight ahead and above me. I am struck by the beauty and strange quality of the light as it approaches. It appears to be a cross in a circle—both are on fire. I walk in that direction and feel fortunate to have this beacon to orient me in the darkness.

Five days before this dream of July 20th, 1978, my mother died unexpectedly. I felt numb with shock and grief as I returned "back home" for the funeral. There I was lost in a sea of memories and sorrow while I helped sort through papers, pictures and other things she had left behind. When I awoke from this dream I felt I had received a mysterious and extraordinary gift. I experienced the awesome light of the circled cross as a sign of divine presence when everything around me seemed shrouded in fog.

Chapter IV

The Practice of Dream Interpretation in the Psychology of Religion

We have seen from the discussion of dream interpretation in historical perspective that dream interpretation has become more democratic, that is, it has moved from the exclusive possession of psychoanalysis and psychotherapy to the domain of personal and spiritual growth for the general public. With the development of humanistic psychology, dream interpretation has also become more participatory, that is the dreamer rather than the analyst or therapist is seen as the ultimate authority on the meaning of his or her dreams. Finally, we have seen that transpersonal psychology has returned to dream interpretation an awareness of transpersonal forces that can influence dream symbols.

These developments have had an impact on dream interpretation in the non-clinical setting.[1] Over the last ten years I have investigated at the University of Toronto the role of dream analysis in the psychology of religion. There we are concerned with the developments described above, namely with the participatory and democratic style of dream interpretation found in humanistic psychology, and with that openness to religious dream interpretations characteristic of transpersonal psychology. In our extracurricular dream seminars we use a method that takes into account 1) the current state of the art of dream interpretation, 2) religious phenomena in dreams and 3) the relation between dream interpretation in the clinical setting and dream interpretation in the non-clinical setting.

In the clinical setting the first concern is for that which "works." For clinical purposes it is enough to interpret dreams at the subjective level and perhaps also at the objective level. In the non-clinical setting of the psychology of religion our concern has been to develop a framework that encompasses both psychological and religious concerns. Here are some guidelines for interpreting dreams in the non-clinical setting, whether in dream groups or as individuals.

Getting Started: Keeping a Dream Journal

Before looking at the rules for interpreting dreams it may be useful to consider how to record and collect your dreams in a journal. A dream journal gives you a permanent record of your dreams so that you can work with them whenever you have a chance. If you also include in your journal any relevant notes on what is happening in your life generally and what you were thinking about before you fell asleep you will be able to return to the context surrounding the dream even months or years later. The dream journal is also the key to unlocking the dream series since only a detailed record of your dreams provides the material necessary for examining the series.

To record dreams you should have pen and paper at your bedside before going to sleep. If you have to get up and search for something to write with when you awake with a dream, you will likely lose part or all of the dream by the time you are ready to write it down. You may wish to use a pen which has its own light or else have a small lamp handy for recording dreams that occur before dawn. Some people prefer using a tape recorder which may permit more detailed recall and less disturbance of the dream atmosphere. The drawback here is that you have to transcribe the dream into your journal later.

Record your dreams when they occur. No matter how vivid a dream seems do not wait until morning or later in the day to put it into your journal. Also record as much detail on colors,

Sample Dream Journal Page

Dream Text:

Associations to the Dream:

Previous day's events, thoughts and general life context:

Themes and main symbols:

Tentative interpretation:

textures, smells, sounds and especially feelings as you can remember. Even small dream fragments are valuable as they may provide clues to the meaning of another dream or a series of dreams. If you have difficulty recalling dreams you may give yourself a suggestion when you are relaxed before falling asleep. Repeat to yourself something simple like: "Tonight I shall remember a dream." Often within a week even low dream recallers report success with this approach.

Your dream journal should also include observations about the general context of your life such as your main concerns and problems. Note any particular events or activities of the day or two preceding a dream. Dreams often incorporate material from recent experience as metaphors for your present life and attitudes. For example, one dreamer watched a baseball game during the day and that night had a dream showing how his life was like coming to bat with the bases loaded and his team behind by three runs in the ninth inning. You might also note what you were thinking about just before falling asleep as dreams frequently comment on our immediate preoccupations.

A loose-leaf folder is ideal for a dream journal because you can always add more material on a particular dream. You should allow space for any associations you have to the various images in the dream. At the bottom of the page you may wish to venture a tentative interpretation bringing together the dream text, your associations to the dream, your life context and events of the previous days. The rules for interpreting dreams set out in this section can guide you in this part of your journal.

The Dream Series

The dream journal is especially valuable in keeping track of the dream series. The dream series is simply a number of dreams taken from the same person whether that be only two, three, or thousands of dreams. To begin with the most elementary form of a dream series, Sigmund Freud holds that all the dreams of a single night deal with the same underlying instinctual impulse. He calls these "homologous dreams."[2] Rollo May broadens this view when he says that all the dreams of the same night refer to the same underlying situation or conflict.[3] Calvin Hall considers the dream series method of analysis to be an important innovation in the study of dreams that has enlarged our understanding of human personality.[4] According to Hall, the more dreams studied, the more accurate and comprehensive is the picture of the dreamer's personality. Carl Jung published extended analyses of dream series that range into the hundreds of dreams.[5]

We can distinguish two general aspects of a dream series. First there is the record of a person's dreams as they occur in chronological order. The dream journal is an excellent way to preserve this *chronological dream series* in permanent form. There is however another aspect to the dream series that becomes apparent after recording a number of dreams. This is the repetition of certain dream themes, characters and symbols. I shall refer to these repeating themes and symbols as the *structural dream series.*

If you organize your journal with an index for the various themes and symbols that recur over the course of many dreams this will help clarify what they mean to you. For example, placing side by side all the dreams where a cat appears gives a good idea of what the symbol "cat" means in your dreams. In this way you are more likely to uncover the meaning of that symbol than if you have just one cat dream to go by.

Various themes such as chase, examination or being late can also be set together to see if there is a pattern to these dreams that might illuminate their meaning. It is also interesting to notice if there are changes in a particular theme as it appears in different dreams since this often reflects developments in your personality. Your dream journal allows you to keep track of both the chronological and structural dream series in as detailed a way as your interest and time permit.

Rules for Interpreting Dreams

These rules apply to both groups and individuals especially where there is an interest in the religious interpretation of dreams. I shall indicate in parentheses the similarities between these rules and the psychological methods described in chapter two.

1) Give the dream a title.
2) Tell the dream in the present tense (Perls).
3) Associate to each dream image (Freud, Jung).
4) Note cultural and mythical associations to the dream (Jung).
5) Note the feelings experienced in relation to dream images and actions (Freud, Jung, Perls).
6) Relate associations to the plot structure (Jung).
7) Highlight and characterize any conflicts present in the dream (Freud, Jung, Perls).
8) Determine subjective or objective reference to the dream (Freud, Jung). Also consider other dimensions of reference.
9) Play-act various elements of the dream (Perls), or use active imagination, i.e. hold a dream image in your mind until it spontaneously changes or speaks (Jung).
10) Attend to the dream series (Freud, Jung, Hall). Also consider a view of the dream series as a symbolic record of the spiritual journey.
11) Draw, paint, sculpt, dance, etc. various dream images, feelings, themes or plots (Jung).

Now I would like to elaborate a bit on each of these rules.

1) *Give a title to the dream.* This helps you identify the main subject of the dream and makes future reference to the dream easier. This is especially useful when you have collected a large number of dreams over a long period of time.

2) *Re-experience the dream in the present.* This allows you to contact the feelings in the dream. These feelings are often valuable guides to the reference and meaning of the dream.

3) *Draw out personal associations to the dream images.* With each of the images in a dream ask what that image means in relation to your own experience. For instance, with the dream of a horse racing toward a lake, the dreamer notes any attitudes

she has toward horses and what a lake means to her.

4) *Note cultural or mythical associations to dream images.* These associations help to broaden the context of the dream. Cultural metaphors symbolize the dynamics of the psyche as well as characterize your relationship to society. Mythical associations relate you to nature, the ancestors and your psychological or spiritual center.

5) *Notice the feelings experienced during various parts of the dream.* These feelings can provide important clues to the meaning of the dream and to which aspects of your life the dream refers.

6) *Relate associations to the plot structure of the dream.* To see how the associations fit together it is necessary to refer the associations back to the dream context. We shall see many examples of this procedure in the illustration following this section.

7) *Highlight and characterize any conflicts present in the dream.* Frequently dreams portray conflicts in your life. They express symbolically the various aspects of these conflicts and may also indicate a way to resolve them.

8) *Determine whether the dream or dream images operate at the subjective or objective levels. Also consider the other dimensions of reference.* The term "dimensions of reference" indicates there are certain dimensions of reality referred to in dreams. Any particular dream may refer to one or more of these dimensions of reality. These dimensions may be classified in any number of ways; I have found this a useful way to list them: 1) the subjective, 2) the objective, 3) the somatic, 4) the telepathic, 5) the archetypal, 6) the spirit world, and 7) the divine. There are also three time dimensions in dreams, namely, the past, the present and the future (precognitive).

The *subjective dimension* pictures the dynamics of a person's mental life. Freud established scientifically the importance of this dimension in *The Interpretation of Dreams*, although subjective aspects of dreams were recognized long before. Freud showed that dreams are not random and meaningless, but are connected to the psychological life. His study of the processes involved in dream formation is a landmark in the scientific study of dreams and especially the subjective dimension of dreams.[6]

A second dimension of dreams is the *objective dimension*. Here dream images refer to realities outside the psyche of the dreamer. The images of people, places and things that appear in dreams may actually be providing another perspective on these realities. This perspective often includes a view of how the subject feels about these external realities at a deep level, nevertheless the image refers to the external world. It is not always clear whether a dream image refers to the real mother or father of the dreamer, for instance, or to the motherly and fatherly aspects of the dreamer's own personality. Distinguishing subjective from objective references is an important part of dream analysis as we noticed in the methods of Freud and Jung.[7]

The *somatic dimension* of the dream is one of the oldest observed. Here dream images portray the dreamer's experience of his or her body. Hippocrates stressed this dimension in diagnosing physical disorders through interpreting dreams.[8] Aristotle considered the somatic dimension of the dream to be its primary reference but he separated his somatic interpretation from the astrological guidelines used by Hippocrates.[9]

A fourth dimension of dream reference is the *telepathic dimension*. In this case dream images refer to what is in the mind of another at a distance, information which we could not know about through ordinary communication channels.[10] While this dimension of dreams is more difficult to comprehend than the other three already discussed, the data indicates the reality of this dimension.[11] The deepest sense of conviction regarding this dimension of dreams comes from carefully observing your own dream experience. This holds true for all of the dimensions of dream reference but your own experience is especially important for taking seriously the paranormal and spiritual dimensions.[12] Many people assume that paranormal experiences such as telepathy, thought-transference, clairvoyance and precognition (which have as yet no known explanation) are somehow spiritual phenomena[13] since the hypothesis of realities extended in space and time needed to account for these phenomena may be related to the spiritual realm.[14]

The *spirit-world* and *divine dimensions* of reference are among the most ancient postulated. As we already noted in chapter one, the Babylonians and Assyrians assumed that bad dreams were caused by spirits of the dead and demons. These spirits were thought to enter dreams and had to be exorcised by means of magic. A special class of priests handled such dream problems in temples dedicated to Makhir, the goddess of dreams. Certain North American Indian tribes reverse the dreamer's relationship to the spirits of the dead: the dreamer's soul journeys to the land of the dead instead of dead spirits visiting the dreamer. The Hopi Indians believe that the dreamer descends into the world of the dead but has nothing to fear if guided by his guardian spirit.[15]

The *divine dimension* of the dream is of central interest to the psychology of religion. According to Morton Kelsey's historical research nearly every major religion of the world has viewed the dream as an important way in which God reveals his will to humans. This is the attitude of the Old Testament, the New Testament and the Church Fathers up until the Middle Ages.[16] By considering the archetypal, the spirit-world and divine dimensions of dream we recognize that the religious aspects of life are frequently represented in dreams and that, for some people, dreams provide a kind of religious experience.

The three time dimensions of dream reference are the past, present and future (precognitive). The *past dimension* refers to those dreams which replay significant or traumatic experiences. These dreams integrate those past experiences with a person's present standpoint in life. Unresolved conflict from the past reemerge as the ego attempts to finish and integrate certain incomplete gestalts. Other dreams include images from the past to show how certain aspects of the dreamer's present circumstances are like persons, places or situations experienced before. Dreams with past reference may even anticipate the future by showing how the outcome of current situations may be similar to what happened in the past situations portrayed. The past dimension of dream reference is frequently therapeutic when it allows a person to re-experience and finish emotional situations thereby freeing up energy for current life experience.

The *present dimension* of dreams is probably the most frequent temporal reference. Dreams synthesize on-going experience by means of symbolic thought. This is seen particularly with the problem-solving and discovery dreams that come as an answer to the dreamer's current questions or difficulties.[17] Everyone who sees dreams primarily as attempts to solve current conflicts works with the present time dimension of dreams. The present dimension of dream reference often portrays the present state of the psyche which is frequently the starting point for psychotherapy. In so far as dreams about present circumstances portray your current experience as religious they may also shed light on your spiritual development.

The *future dimension* of dream reference is, like the telepathic dimension, one of the most difficult to comprehend from our conscious perspective on time and space. How the dreaming mind can extend into the future is a difficult question to answer.[18] We still have to deal with the fact of precognition in dreams even though we do not yet possess the theoretical principles to explain exactly how such experiences occur, just as with telepathic dreams. According to Ullman's studies, precognition regarding the dreamer's future is the most frequent type of spontaneous paranormal dream.[19] He states that the majority of precognitive dreams are about death, disaster and danger, which supports Jung's view that these phenomena tend to occur in archetypal situations. The future (precognitive) dimension of dream reference is rarely highlighted in the clinical setting but in the psychology of religion we attend to the many reports of precognitive dreams in the literature on dreams and in the experience of dreamers in our courses. In any setting where people attend to their dreams, whether clinical or non-clinical, they are more likely to notice precognition in their dreams.

You can apply any or all of these dimensions to your dreams as hypotheses to be tested. A hypothetical perspective is considered productive or "correct" if it 1) leads to an insight for the dreamer, 2) permits various elements of a dream to fall into place, 3) fits in with other dreams in the series, 4) squares with observations on other aspects of the dreamer's life and 5) helps to move the dreamer's life (attitudes and actions) in a positive direction. If applying an interpretive hypothesis achieves one or more of these criteria then the hypothesis can be considered valid in that case. Considering these various dimensions of reference relates your dreams to your life experience.

9) *Play-act various dream images and/or use active imagination with parts of the dream. Also bring into dialogue certain figures of the dream.* This can be done in the dreamer's mind or in the form of a written dialogue as active imagination (Jung); or it can be done by play-acting the encounter, i.e. shuttling back and forth between the characters, play-acting one, then the other, to create a dialogue (Perls).

10) *Consider the dream series (chronological and structural series). Also consider a view of the dream series as a symbolic record of the spiritual journey.* The psychotherapist usually focuses on those elements in the series that are useful to therapy as defined by a particular psychological theory. For example, Freudians tend to focus on those dreams or aspects of dreams that deal with conflicts of sex and aggression. Jungians tend to focus on those parts of the dream series that manifest archetypal constellations. Gestalt therapists tend to focus on polarity conflicts in dreams.[20] These various therapeutic approaches to the dream series are best understood as working hypotheses that are applied provisionally in order to see if they illuminate the meaning of dreams. Verification of such interpretive hypotheses is found primarily in their effect on the dreamer in the same way you verify any of the dimensions of reference for a single dream.

You might also apply a religious interpretive hypothesis to the dream series. According to such an hypothesis the dream series can be considered the symbolic story of your life or the symbolic record of your spiritual journey. This story encompasses those aspects that are therapeutically useful as well as all other aspects of dreams. From this perspective the therapeutic use of dreams can be considered as a "clinical episode" within the larger story of the total dream series. It is the total dream series that is the symbolic record of a person's spiritual journey.

11) *Draw, paint, sculpt, dance, etc. various dream images.* This is a way to sink more deeply into the mood of a dream, to

explore some of the more powerful or obscure symbols and also to dream the dream onward in your imagination. The meaning or reference of a dream may also emerge for the first time during these activities.

Eight Good Books on Dream Interpretation

To supplement this section on rules for interpreting your own dreams I would like to add a short list of useful books to read. These are practical, non-technical, books that elaborate on the rules suggested here and offer other perspectives on interpreting your dreams.

G. Delaney, *Living Your Dreams*
A. Faraday, *The Dream Game*
A. Faraday, *Dream Power*
C. Hall, *The Meaning of Dreams*
C. Hall and V. Nordby, *The Individual and His Dreams*
R. Johnson, *Inner Work*
M. Ullman and N. Zimmerman, *Working with Dreams*
S. Williams, *Jungian-Senoi Dreamwork Manual*

The best way to verify for yourself the usefulness of these rules is to try them out. You can benefit by applying any or all of these rules to your own dreams. Here I would add that as effective and rewarding as individual dream interpretation can be, there are additional benefits in group work. The principal advantages to group work are: 1) emotional support, i.e. you are not the only person in the world with strange dreams; 2) insights into your own problems and creativity as you see how others deal with their dreams; 3) the relatively low cost of group work as compared to individual psychotherapy; 4) camaraderie and creative atmosphere of the dream group; 5) more incentive to work on your own dreams; 6) increased sensitivity to your own dream life, i.e. dream recall frequently improves with the group involvement; and 7) more practice with dream language.

Like any other language, proficiency in dream language increases with use. Practice creates a certain "fluency" and the dream group provides a creative atmosphere in which to practice understanding this language. Many find they can work on their own dreams much faster and with better results when they are involved in group work. In the rest of this chapter I shall present an example of how these rules work when applied in a dream group.

Notes

1. A non-clinical setting for dream interpretation means any setting where psychotherapy is not the primary concern; dream groups, schools, churches and families are some typical non-clinical settings.
2. Sigmund Freud, *The Interpretation of Dreams, SE* IV, p. 334.
3. Rollo May and Leopold Caligor, *Dreams and Symbols* (New York, 1968), p. 43.
4. Calvin Hall, *The Meaning of Dreams,* (New York, 1966), p. 2.
5. See Jung's "Individual Dream Symbolism in Relation to Alchemy," (*CW* 12, pp. 39-223) and *The Visions Seminars* (Zuerich, 1976).
6. As we saw in the second chapter, Fritz Perls, a founder of Gestalt therapy, held an extreme position on the subjective dimension of dreams. He stated that each image in a dream is an aspect of the dreamer's own personality (*Gestalt Therapy Verbatim* (Moab, Utah, 1974), p. 71). While this is an extremely productive assumption in therapy, its reductionist formulation does not allow for the possibility that dream images might refer simultaneously to aspects of the dreamer's personality as well as to realities outside of the dreamer's psyche or that images might simply refer to other external realities with no reference at all to the dreamer's personality.
7. There is no *a priori* reason for eliminating the possibility that dreams refer to elements in the external world. One dream investigator, Ann Faraday, insists that this objective (literal) reference of dream images is the first possibility that should be tested. Because the unconscious psyche may pick up on characteristics of people and situations that the conscious mind misses, the objective dimension of dreams can contribute to our awareness of and relationship to these people and situations. Consequently the objective dimension can be considered therapeutically significant. The objective dimension can also deal with spiritual matters if the dream images refer to religious objects or spiritual people and places.
8. In Hippocrates' view a dream reflecting what normally happens in nature (regarding the weather, cycles of growth, the sun, moon and planets) means that the body is healthy. Dream images of irregularities in nature or

the planets mean that there is a problem in the corresponding microcosmic body system. For instance, drought pictured in a dream might indicate anemia; flooding could indicate high blood pressure. Galen repeats this kind of somatic interpretation based on the analogy of the microcosm (the body) and the macrocosm (the world).

9. For Aristotle a dream represented the residual movements of the senses left over from waking. Most dreams were, in this view, a random replay of impressions from the previous day's activities. However, the dream could also indicate the body's condition during sleep since attention is withdrawn from the external world and focused on internal stimuli which might reflect a somatic disorder and possibly its prognosis. According to Carl Meier, the Greek focus on the somatic dimension, i.e. the diagnostic, prognostic and therapeutic role of dreams, tended to limit the scope of dreams. See "The Dream in Ancient Greece and Its Use in Temple Cures," in *The Dream and Human Societies*, ed. E. von Grunebaum (Los Angeles, 1966), p. 314. Morton Kelsey traces much of the modern critical attitude toward dreams as a natural, random and basically meaningless activity back to an exaggerated Aristotelianism which became the dominant attitude in Western culture (especially through the influence of St. Thomas Aquinas and the Church). The somatic dimension came to be identified with the primary meaning (or lack of meaning) of dreams. This was the position of the late 19th-century medical world criticized by Freud for dealing with dreams "with the sole aim of applying its physiological theories" to dreams (*Introductory Lectures on Psychoanalysis* (*SE* XV) p. 86) and for concluding that dreams as a reflection of somatic processes are useless or down-right pathological.

10. Frederic Meyers, who coined this term in 1882, defined telepathy as "fellow feeling at a distance." The telepathic dimension is also closely related to the phenomenon of clairvoyance which refers to events at a distance which are felt or seen directly although they are not necessarily transmitted from someone else's mind.

11. Montague Ullman, a long-time researcher in this area, indicates the three major sources of evidence for this dimension of dream reference as: 1) published accounts of spontaneous telepathy that have been carefully investigated and documented by reliable observers, 2) accounts by psychiatrists and therapists of patients' telepathic dreams and 3) the production of telepathic dreams in the laboratory. The laboratory studies on dream telepathy carried out by Ullman and others at the Maimonides Medical Center in New York attempt to confirm experimentally this elusive dimension of dreams. Ullman's book, *Dream Telepathy,* provides a convincing record of the results in this area. The lack of explanatory principles to account for the data certainly does not preclude the reality of the phenomena themselves.

12. According to Carl Jung, such phenomena as telepathy, precognition and clairvoyance are most likely to occur under the following conditions: 1)

there is some emotional tie between the persons involved in the experience, 2) an archetypal situation is involved, such as death or an accident, and 3) there is an open attitude to the possibility of such paranormal phenomena. Ullman also emphasized that an open-minded attitude is especially important in the experimental induction of telepathic dreams.

13. Mircea Eliade cites a number of examples of the paranormal powers such as clairvoyance, precognition and thought-reading that are ascribed to shamans and medicine men in various tribes and religions (*Myths, Dreams and Mysteries* (New York, 1975), p. 87). The precognitive aspect of prophecy in the Judaeo-Christian tradition also suggests this connection between the paranormal and the spiritual dimensions of dreams.

14. John Sanford suggests in *Dreams, God's Forgotten Language* that man's religious instincts may be partly founded on the unconscious perception of an invisible reality which underlies conscious existence (p. 67). Whether such hypothetical realities coincide to some degree with the spirit world or the divine cannot be answered with certainty. Nevertheless, the common characteristic of extending beyond conscious space-time categories of here and now is enough to link the telepathic to the spirit-world and divine dimensions of dream reference in the minds of some.

15. We also find this dimension of dreams in the Algonquin tribe. They cite cases where in extreme illness, the dreamer's spirit travelled to the land of the dead and reanimated the body upon return.

16. I have already mentioned in chapter one the reasons Kelsey gives for the decreasing importance of the divine dimension of dreams in Western Christianity. These early trends devaluing dreams were reinforced in the 18th century, the Age of Reason and Enlightenment, when "educated people" derided any claim to prophecy or communication with another world through dreams.

17. Thomas French and Erika Fromm underscore this aspect of dreams in their "focal conflict" theory of dreams. See *Dream Interpretation: A New Approach* (New York, 1964). According to their view the central and immediate preoccupations of the dreamer are attended to in symbolic form. In their method, the analyst scans dream content to locate the dreamer's current problem. While they also state that the present focal conflict can be traced back to conflicts in the dreamer's past, the "precipitating stimulus" of dreams is in the present.

18. J.W. Dunne's work, *An Experiment With Time*, is one attempt to formulate a theoretical solution to this problem.

19. Paranormal dreams involve telepathy, clairvoyance or precognition.

20. This is not only a matter of the therapist's expectations and attention to particular dream elements, but also of the patient's unconscious arrangement of dream symbols. Patients tend to dream in patterns that are consistent with the theoretical orientation of the therapist. This often-observed phenomenon, called "doctrinal compliance," means that Freudian patients tend to have Freudian dreams, Jungian patients tend to have

Jungian dreams, etc. See J. Ehrenwald, *The ESP Experience: A Psychiatric Validation* (New York, 1978), pp. 56-62. Whether it is due to the therapist's orienting perspective or to the patient's unconscious compliance, there is a certain selection from the dream series of material that is useful in therapy. This conscious or unconscious selection of material from the dream series greatly influences the therapeutic interpretation of dreams.

Illustrative Case: A Dream Seminar

In this section we shall consider an example of how the rules of dream interpretation work in a group setting. This dream seminar is an extracurricular group[1] composed of about ten people. A member of the group volunteers to work on a dream. He or she tells the dream in the present tense as if the action were taking place now. The other members of the seminar listen to the dream; some take notes.

The dreamer usually includes in the initial telling any feelings that may have been part of the dream and comments about what was happening the day before the dream. She may also add any feelings that emerge while telling the dream to the group or remarks about major concerns and preoccupations in her life. Any of the others may then raise questions as well as make observations about the dream symbols. The first round of questions usually elicits the dreamer's associations to the main dream symbols. A central question we keep in mind throughout the entire process is: How does this dream story relate to the present life circumstances of the dreamer?

The "authority of the dreamer" guides the interpretive work in that the dreamer has the power to accept or reject an interpretation. At any point the dreamer may say that a certain line of interpretation does not fit the dream. This curtails those in the group who may wish to impose their own agenda or theories on a particular dream. It also provides a safety valve for groups not under the supervision of a trained analyst. The dreamer can reject an interpretation which may be close to the point but is too painful or emotional to deal with in such unsupervised or informal conditions. Resistances should be respected.

Here I would like to illustrate this method by describing a session in which we interpret the dream of William, a student in his final year of undergraduate studies at the University of Toronto.[2] William begins telling his dream:

Snakes and Ladder

I am walking down to the ravine by Summerhill Avenue, with my father in front of two unknown young men of about my age. One of them has dark longish hair which is unkempt. I do not recall how the other looks. As we descend down into the ravine, I learn that the guy with the long hair also lives on Summerhill Avenue. I ask him on which side of Mt. Pleasant (the street beside the ravine which interrupts or divides Summerhill Avenue) he lives on. He answers vaguely. I point and say: "On the side near the tracks or the one with the dead end?" Realizing that this could describe either side, I point to the Rosedale side and he agrees. I say: "Oh well, I live on that side" (pointing to the Yonge Street side).

He finds a folding pocket knife with a wooden handle and throws it into a railroad tie. I say that I guess if you've been down here long enough you learn to use one of those things. He says it was a fluke really because the knife was so crummy. I figure that it had belonged to some rubby (i.e. wino). I notice that it wobbles so I don't take it.

The surroundings now become more lush and tropical. It is a huge jungle. In the middle of it is an enormous wooden ladder which goes up, up, up. I don't recall seeing the top to it though there may have been one. It disappears into a fog or clouds.

I find an identical pocket knife and look for somewhere to throw it. The guy with unkempt hair holds up a small wooden board over his chest as a target but I laugh saying that would be very stupid! I then think to hit the ladder. I forget exactly where I threw it but it sticks well into the target. The other guy is impressed. I also complain that the knife was cheap. Then I come across a very good kitchen knife on the ground. It has a wooden handle (but now I am unsure that it is not cheap). I pick it up and we continue walking.

As I approach the ladder I notice a snake on the path below me. I stop to allow him to pass. I am relieved that I saw him. But to my surprise another snake is coming down the ladder. I realize that if I stop for the first, the second will descend and get me. I panic but am frozen to the spot.

I have a BB gun in a stapler and attempt to shoot the snake. I wonder if I should use the kitchen knife but figure it would be too messy. I shoot the snake but hit him only in the body. This does not stop him. I think he may bite me when he squirms in pain. He is *really* close. I shoot again and again but still he descends. I cannot move. I awake in a panic. That's the dream. Weird, eh?

Bob: Does the ravine near Summerhill Avenue mean anything to you?

Wm.:   Yes. The ravine played a large part in my childhood. It was how I could get to school by shortcut. However my mother strictly forbade the children from using it because it was rumored to contain winos and child molesters . . . . I guess in Freudian terms, the shape and plant growth suggest a vagina and pubic hair. Hmmm . . . the ravine is a natural wooded area in the middle of the city. Nature suggests to me the realm of the unconscious, as does the fact that the ravine is lower than the rest of this city.

This ravine also separated me from my Rosedale schoolmates. I came from the wrong side of the tracks so I was unacceptable in the eyes of my peers. Here I imagine it represents my own fears that sexuality is not respectable.

Jane: What about the people with you: your father and the other two unknown figures?

Wm.:   Yes, I am following my father down and down is the direction of the unconscious. This could suggest that this is an area where I see my father as a model or leader, i.e. in sexuality, but also maturity in every respect. The two young men are probably my brothers, Tom and Steve. They too live on Summerhill Avenue and are "about my age." The young man with unkempt hair also suggests my brother's friend, Peter Young. I do not like him but my brother Steve has a tendency to be like him, unkempt hair, etc.

Margaret: The name of your brother's friend, Peter Young,

suggests that this part of the dream may be referring to a time in your life when you and Steve were "young," i.e. your childhood.

Howard: Or that this personality characteristic, being unkempt, may be a "young," i.e. underdeveloped or unrecognized part of you.

Wm.: Yeah, that's good. I do see the young man with the long hair as a shadow figure—unruly, unkempt, dark, having some of the same qualities I find distasteful in my brother Steve. The fact that he lives on *the other side* of Summerhill Ave. also suggests he is my shadow.[3]

Brigid: Does the wobbly knife remind you of anything?

Wm.: Yes. Of course, the knife is a familiar symbol for the phallus. The unkempt young man finding the pocket knife suggests to me a semi-erect or erecting penis. Perhaps this refers to the first time I saw my brother Steve with a morning "hard on" and became aware of sexual prowess. The three of us brothers shared a bedroom from birth to fourteen years of age.

Bob: If we're going to stick to Freudian symbolism then wood is a female symbol and railway ties lie on their back and are run over by the phallic train. This suggests to me that sticking the knife into the wood tie is a fairly explicit reference to the sex act.

Wm.: Or since he alone throws the knife, perhaps it refers to masturbation, an act I was more likely to witness in our shared bedroom. Regardless, I complement him on his prowess and remark that if one stays "down here"—in the forbidden garden of sexuality—one becomes adept at sex. Still I am repulsed by the phallic symbol, thinking that it must belong to a wino or rubby—that vague category for dirty, homosexual or perverse impulses.

Peter: If this imagery is sexual in the dream, then the first exposure to sex causes the surroundings to become much more plush and tropical. Since such vegetation often symbolizes pubic hair, this suggests the emerg-

Barb:
In any event the vegetation becomes more alive and luxurious. This seems to be a positive development until the snake appears.

Jane:
I think the pocket knife could well be a phallic symbol but it may represent more. Its blade penetrates when it is thrown into the railroad tie. Since the tie belongs properly to the bridge (the "tie" between the ego and the unconscious elements) then hitting this tie suggests that the shadow side has struck the conscious/unconscious boundary through the emergence of sexual prowess. The initiative, drive or first awareness is in the unconscious and not the ego.

Margaret:
Along these same lines, once this shadow makes contact with the ego, life begins to quicken, the forest becomes more plush and larger. This suggests sexual excitement. But moving past Freudian symbols, it could also be the enriching of elan vital, the life force. Hence the shadow has a certain creative, life-giving power, which though it disgusts you at first, must be reowned.

Wm.:
Yes, that's good. The pocket knife definitely represents more than just the sexual. It has a penetrating power which is both sexual and psychological. I wonder where to make contact with this knife. The shadow figure holds a board up to his chest, inviting some kind of contact. I'm afraid that this is foolhardy. I think to make contact with the ladder. In confusion I forget exactly what I hit, but I know that the blade has stuck into the target well and the shadow figure is impressed. I guess this could suggest that an early experimental attempt at making contact with the unconscious through sexuality was successful but the exact circumstances are not recalled.

Helen:
There's also the larger kitchen knife. What about that?

ing awareness of puberty with the first appearance of pubic hair.

Wm.:   The kitchen knife is good but I doubt its value. With it I have a better tool to penetrate the unconscious but again I'm unsure of its worth, hesitant to "trust its blade." To me this shows a deeper mistrust of the whole enterprise. Even with this encouraging find, I manage to remain doubtful.

Susan: The ladder image is fascinating. In the middle of this lush natural setting it is a strange, almost otherworldly image.

Wm.:   It *is* a remarkable image. Suddenly the main feature of the ravine becomes the enormous wooden ladder, plunging from the sky, past the lush plants and into the moist, dark and fertile earth. (Laughter) Talk about phallic . . . . The ladder is ancient and has been left there by an archaic tribe of primitives. It reminds me of the Aztec temples: it has a magic and serenity all of its own. It is rooted in the fertile earth and reaches up to the clouds. It seems like a magical and ancient transformation symbol—a way to move from earth to heaven.

Susan: This whole image reminds me of something I read by William Irwin Thompson about Quetzlcoatl, the Mexican myth of a snake who climbs up a tree trunk to become a bird.[4] He says that this snake-tree-bird iconography is almost universal and represents a transformation from flesh to spirit. Thompson sees a parallel to the staff, the caduceus, of the Roman god Mercury. Going further back to Greek mythology, Hermes with his two entwined serpents and phallus was a fertility symbol. Yet this fertility is not simply biological. Hermes is also a messenger, a god of the crossroads and the leader of souls to and from the underworld. His phallus penetrates from the known into the unknown. Not only are the two snakes of Hermes present in this dream but also the penetration of the "penis" or knife blade, being both a sexual and spiritual reference.

Wm: Yes! That's amazingly close. Though I've never

studied mythology before, those myths seem to contain all my dream elements. (Pause) Except that instead of "deliverance," I feel that the snake traps me, glues me to the spot. I know that the two snakes entwined on a staff is a common symbol of healing, like the emblem of the Canadian Medical Association. But instead of "healing," I feel the snake on the ladder will be deadly or poisonous, the exact opposite of healing.

Bob: No, I prefer the Freudian explanation we were working towards. Let's keep the snake as a phallic symbol. In that context your paralysis could mean you were afraid to follow your father into normal sexual development.

Wm.: You mean because I fear the incestuous and homosexual possibilities represented by my brothers? Yes . . . And the snake was coming *down* the ladder so the two would entwine on the ground instead of on the staff. That's the opposite of the Mercury or Quetzlcoatl myths you were talking about, Susan.

Susan: Well let's ask why this transformation symbol became one of entrapment?

Wm.: You mean, why has the healing symbol become poisonous?

Howard: Hey let's get real here. How about applying this mythical interpretation to your life?

Wm.: Well, my initial reaction to puberty was one of disavowal. I simply did not allow it to affect me. Given my strict "old country" family atmosphere and my Roman Catholic education, I saw sexuality and the awakening of my own phallic powers as threatening or "dirty." The spirit was important and questions about the flesh would wait until that vague future event, "marriage." In reality, my conscious sexual development came to a halt just as my progress comes to a halt in my dream. I refused to own the snake on the ground, be it my penis, sexuality or this-worldliness. This brings the snake from the heavens down the ladder. (Pause) . . . To me the message seems clear: there is to be no spiritual transformation as long as I do not deal with the flesh.

Jane: In reaction to the second snake you attempt to shoot him with a BB gun in a stapler. What do you make of this strange image?

Wm.:   The image of a shooting gun is obviously phallic. "BB" suggests to me "baby" which could refer to the young penis which shoots only small bullets or to the penis' procreational function. I also owned a BB gun in my early puberty. Not only was it a hobby which allowed me to escape sexuality, it was probably a phallic substitute as well. I also associate the stapler with school work and essays. I guess this could mean that I transferred my attention from my sexual development to my school work. (Pause).

Oh wait! Now I remember! We used to play a game at Our Lady of Perpetual Help grade school. I would pass through the ravine to get to this school. We would play-act the episodes of the television series 'Star Trek' with each boy taking on the role of a cast member like Spock or McCoy. We would steal staplers from the teacher's desk to use as phasers, the ray-gun weapons. With this phaser gun, you could disintegrate your opponent as I try to do to the snake.

Ah yes! This act of annihilation is indeed an act of "*dis*-integration." That's a pun on the term for reowning shadow elements! The opposite of "integration" is *dis*-integration. What a good pun!

Instead of hitting the snake in the head, which I know is the only way to kill it (a lesson I learned from many statues of Jesus and Mary crushing the head of the serpent), I shoot him in the body, again an act of penetration into the shadowy flesh. But this method is ineffective in stopping the snake and threatens to cause him to bite me.

While on one level this may refer to masturbation it also seems to be a symbol for my attempt to penetrate the shadow side of life. I guess that masturbation is a rehearsal for entry into the world of sexuality. Yet it is an ineffective way to penetrate the mysteries of the flesh. I even think to use the kitchen knife to cut the snake open but am afraid of the mess. The knife would bring the bloody interior of the shadow figure into full view, which would be too repulsive. Yet there I stand paralyzed and so close to being poisoned.

Howard: I think the dream is saying that spirituality and this world of flesh are inseparable. In this dream the stuff of this world, the wooden ladder, the snakes and the plants become symbols of spiritual transformation. This dream suggests that your method for dealing with the flesh is one of dis-integration and therefore anti-spiritual. It seems you have to reown the flesh for spiritual transformation.

Wm.: This idea is definitely not encouraged in our society or in my religious upbringing. In fact I was taught that to further spiritual growth, you have to arrest physical desires or concerns of the flesh. This dream tells me that I have introjected and lived by this mistaken idea. By refusing to take the flesh seriously, spiritual transformation becomes poison.

In an effort to understand the dream more fully William also play-acted some of the main dream elements. He uses the subjective hypothesis, assuming that each of these images refers to an aspect of his own personality. Here are some portions from that work and William's observations on that work:

William as the ravine: "I am the ravine, somewhat wild but also cultivated. I am a wild forest in the middle of the city. I am somewhat dangerous. There are winos, rubbies and muggers in me. (Pause) . . . But I am also a very nice park. I have beautiful trees, a river. My soil is good. I may be an inconvenience to William because I separate him from school and I otherwise interrupt traffic, but I also serve a purpose. People come and play in me and go away refreshed . . . . I'm also solid enough to hold up this bridge to get trains across . . . . (In a deeper voice:) Now I am more lush, more wild. See my beautiful exotic plants. My soil is moist, warm and dark. I give life. I love life and growth."

Wm. as his father: "Come on guys. I'm leading the way. Down here. Follow me. Isn't this a great ravine. It's so nice to be hiking in the woods. This is familiar ground. This is easy."

Wm. as Peter Young: "I'm a tough guy, see. I've been down here all my life. I can do anything. Watch this knife shot. Thunk! Not bad eh? and that was with a cheap blade. My Dad's got loads of dough so I do what I want. But I like it down here where it's tough."

Wm. as the other young man: "I'm just following along. I'm so unimportant, I don't have a name. I don't even have a face."

Wm.:   How often I feel like these characters! I especially can re-own the characters of these two young men, the self-assured, tough-talking but essentially hollow wise guy and the faceless droid who just follows along. At different times I act like both of these guys. One seems to be the opposite of the other. I also relate to my father's love of the outdoors and his tendency to lead. The ravine is at once terrible and beautiful, frightening and life-giving. It is also mostly wild but has been cultivated or polluted to some extent. This would describe my life, I think.

Wm. as the bridge: "I am concrete. I am big and strong. Nothing can knock me down. I'm useful. My main job is to allow the train to cross over the ravine. A train can go across me and I don't even feel it. No sweat, no strain. Here comes the train but I won't feel it because I'm solid, solid concrete."

Wm. as the pocket knife: "I used to be nice and useful but I was lost by some kid. Now I'm a little shabby and wobbly . . . . But look I still work! I stick into this railroad tie pretty good. My blade is still in good shape. If you could get a new handle on me, and polish me up a little I could be a useful tool for cutting things."

Wm. as the railroad tie: "Hey! Why did you poke me? . . . I guess it's okay. A little knife like that can't hurt. I don't know *what* I'm doing down here. I belong properly up there on the bridge as a support for the trains. Down here I'm a totem pole."

Wm. as the ladder: (Deep voice) "I'm big and ancient. My steps are for giants. I am as old as humanity, from the days of the giants. My feet run deep into this warm moist soil and my head goes way up into the clouds. I'm old and weathered. Nothing could knock me down."

Wm.:   The concrete bridge supports train tracks which sug-
         gest a "drive," a power drive of some kind. The
         rigidity of the bridge suggests how my back feels
         when studying. The drive (i.e. train) is for success in
         school. The pocket knife suggests a tool of penetra-
         tion I had when I was younger but have now dis-
         carded. This dream image suggests that its blade is
         still good but the handle needs to be changed, i.e. I
         should change the way I handle it. I guess the railroad
         tie is a part of myself which I normally use to support
         my power drives (the drive of the train engine) but
         now serves a very different purpose when in touch
         with the life-giving earth. It is now a totem pole; it
         serves a deeply religious purpose now. This religious
         theme is carried over to the ladder which is also an-
         chored in the earth but reaches up to the heavens. If *I*
         am the ladder, the tie and the tool to make contact,
         then in this realm I begin to make some contact with
         the religious forces within myself. These religious
         forces are both immanent (the totem pole which em-
         bodies this-worldly gods) and transcendent (the
         ladder).

Now William enacts a dialogue to deal with the unresolved conflicts in this dream. In the path ahead he comes across a large black snake. Here is their interaction:

Snake: Hisssss. Ahhhh. I like it here on the cool brown earth and in the hot sun. Yesssss. I live in this ravine and it is good to me. It gives me many rodents to eat. But I am on this path first. If you step on me, watch out! I am poisonous when I want to be. But if you don't bother me, I won't bother you. I'll just keep eating and sunning and crawling.

Wm.: Let me pass snake. I want to join my father and the others.

Snake: No I got here first. I have as much right to this path as you. This ravine is my home. You better not come near me! Hisss.

Wm.: Oh no! Here comes another snake down the ladder! Please let me go through. *Please*.

Snake: No. This is my spot. You have a whole ravine. Go around me.

Wm.: No. I must keep on the path! I have to follow my father down the beaten path. The rest of this jungle is wild. I could get lost. Or worse. There are *snakes* in this jungle you know!

Snake: Yesss. I noticed. But it seems to me (and I class myself an expert witness in this case) that there are also snakes on the path.

Wm.: But you can at least see them on the path. The path is safer.

Snake: Well it doesn't seem to be working out that way for you, bucko! Look beside you.

Wm.: From this dialogue with the snake I learn that I am the hedonist, the natural snake who takes his pleasure in the simple fruits of life. This is in conflict with another force which wishes to follow the beaten path because of an unreasonable fear of the jungle (unreasonable since the dangers I *believe* to be hidden there are already manifest on the path). These two opposites have to be brought closer together. I see how I have alienated this part of me which wishes to live fully and in this world.

I also feel how inhibited I really am. How I refuse to leave the beaten path. How I refuse to take chances. It is this inhibition which stops me from making any contact with my natural self—the growing, alive ravine.

Finally, William does a drawing of the Snake and Ladder dream. Here is his drawing and the thoughts that came to him while working on it:

Wm.:   While drawing the pencil outline I realized that I had
drawn everything except myself. When it came time
to color in the drawing I had some difficulty finding
room for me. This suggests a resistance to being seen
involved in earthy (sexual) things.

As I was sketching the ladder I was struck by
a thought about the biblical story of Jacob who
dreamed that he saw God's angels ascending and
descending a ladder from heaven to earth. Like
Jacob's ladder, my dream ladder reaches into the
heavens. But instead of an angel of God, a snake
descends! In the Garden of Eden, Lucifer, God's
brightest (and proudest) angel takes the form of a
snake. This suggests to me when an angel becomes
flesh I can only see it as evil. I am very afraid of this
snake. I do not see that it is in fact from God, that
what it represents, this-worldly matter, flesh, is also
from God. I have created or acquired a dualism
which associates this world with evil.

I stopped painting for a minute and found my
Bible. I looked for the passage with Jacob's ladder in
it. After Jacob's dream he said, "Surely the Lord is
in this place, and I did not know it . . . How awesome
is this place! This is none other than the house of
God, and this is the gate of heaven." (Gen.
28:16-17). For me this is a very powerful passage. If I
am the ravine then I am the holy ground in which
"Jacob's ladder" is rooted. This means the Self is
"the house of God." This ties in with a Christian
doctrine I learned very early at school, that each of us
is a "temple" in which the Holy Spirit dwells. This
ravine, the Self as total organism—*the body as holy
ground*—is where God lives.

From this example of working on William's dream we can
see how the rules of dream interpretation work in a group setting. Now I would like to relate these rules even more explicitly
to the preceding discussion and work.

1) *Give a title to the dream.* This helps the dreamer to identify the main subject of his dream and makes future reference to the dream easier. His title, "Snakes and Ladder," may also help to identify themes in a series of dreams. This name, which William derived from a childhood boardgame, "Snakes and Ladders," was particularly useful because it reminded him of major symbols and childhood, a major theme.

2) *Re-experience the dream in the present.* William tells the dream in the present tense. If any parts of the dream are unclear, members may ask him to repeat segments of the dream. Some of the members take notes on the dream as William tells it; others prefer to rely on their memories and attend more to the way the dream is told.

3) *Draw out personal associations to the dream images.* After William tells the dream, members ask about various elements of the dream. They may choose any element that strikes them as particularly interesting or important. Bob asks about the first major image of the dream, the ravine, but he might have begun with any image. At this stage it is a matter of drawing out personal associations William has to the dream elements, namely the ravine, the father, the two young men, the snakes, the bridge, the pocket knife, the railroad tie and the ladder.

4) *Note cultural or mythical associations to dream images.* Group members may note associations that occur to them as they listen. Margaret's suggestion that the dream character, Peter Young, may be referring to the time when William was a *young* boy draws upon the cultural associations in language. When Susan reflects upon the similarity between the snake and ladder dream image and the Hermes and Quetzlcoatl myths she is drawing upon mythical associations to broaden the context of William's dream. Such cultural and mythical associations do not override the dreamer's personal associations but they may shed light on certain aspects of a dream image. In this case the myths draw attention to the transformational possibilities portrayed in the dream.

5) *Notice the feelings experienced during various parts of the dream.* While telling the dream William notes feelings of relief, satisfaction, surprise, fear and panic that he experienced during

the dream. These feelings provide clues both to the meaning of the dream and to which aspects of William's life the dream refers.

6) *Relate associations to the plot structure of the dream.* To see how the associations fit together it is necessary to refer the associations back to the dream context. In this case William associates the phallus with the knives, so he considers this dream as a picture of his attitude toward sex. The knife was "crummy," wobbly and probably belonged to a wino; this reflects William's attitude toward the penis as something suspect and dirty. The fact that the unkempt boy discovers the first knife further emphasizes this negative portrait of William's attitude toward sex.

7) *Highlight and characterize any conflicts present in the dream.* The major conflicts in this dream involve: a) William and the unkempt young man, b) William and the knives, and c) William and the snakes and the ladder. All of these conflicts revolve around William's attitudes toward sexuality and spiritual transformation in a way that offers hope of integrating these two areas of William's life.

8) *Determine whether the dream or dream images operate at the subjective or objective levels. Also consider the transpersonal dimensions of reference* (described in the first half of this chapter). William sees some of the dream images at the objective level, (i.e. referring to people in the outer world) and some at the subjective level, (i.e. referring to aspects of his own personality). The father in his dream refers to his actual father who led the way in his attitude toward sexuality (the objective level); the father may also refer to that part of William that is like his father and sticks to the path (the subjective level). The Peter Young character is interpreted primarily at the subjective level, representing William's own unruly and tough tendencies. The knives and snakes are seen as metaphors representing William's sexuality.

There are also two transpersonal dimensions of reference that may illuminate William's dream. The snake-ladder imagery appears to have mythical (archetypal) connections to the Hermes and Quetzlcoatl myths. The mythical reference places this dream in the context of spiritual transformation through the "earthly," an ancient motif that sheds light on William's dream.

The divine dimension is suggested by William's associations as he sketched the ladder. He thought about Jacob's ladder and how the snakes of his dream may represent communication from the divine through an earthly vehicle, namely, matter and the flesh. William saw the dream as referring to his relationship with God in a surprising way. He saw the body (as the ravine) revealed to be holy ground.

9) *Play-act various dream images and/or use active imagination with parts of the dream.* In this example we see William identifying with the major images in the dream. Through this process he is able to experience how characteristics of the dream images express aspects of his own personality. For instance, he becomes aware of how often he feels like the father leading the way or the unkempt young man with a tough front or the docile follower. In play-acting the ravine he senses his wildness and his connection with nature. By enacting the dialogue between himself and the snake, he comes to recognize the conflict between his desire to enjoy the natural side of life and his fear of the flesh. He might also have done this dialogue as active imagination, that is, merely carrying on the dialogue in his mind or writing it out rather than play-acting it.

10) *Relate the dream to the dreamer's life. Interpret the dream as you would a picture of the dreamer's personality.* William sees this dream as a dramatic representation of his early attitudes toward sex that still influence his thinking and behavior. He recognizes the influences of his family and Catholic education in shaping his attitude to the relationship between spiritual and sexual matters. He sees the dream as calling into question what he learned, namely that spiritual development requires a denial of sex, the flesh or the material world. The dream pictures this personality conflict as a confrontation between William and the snakes. By showing the snake coming down the ladder the dream provides an unexpected perspective, that spiritual truth may be communicated through the earthly.

11) *Consider the dream series. Also consider a view of the*

dream series as a symbolic record of the spiritual journey.
William refers the snake image to many of his other dreams
where the snake is clearly a phallic symbol. This increases the
likelihood that in this dream the snake also represents the
phallus or sexuality. As we saw in the last section the repeated
images of the snake represent part of the structural dream
series. Other dreams preceding and following this dream (*the
chronological dream series*) also deal with the motif of searching
for a viable spirituality and life-style. This tends to confirm the
"spirituality-sexuality" interpretation of this dream. This
dream can be considered as part of a symbolic record of
William's attitude toward sex in relationship to spiritual
transformation. William's associations to Jacob's ladder also
add to a spiritual interpretation of the dream series.

12) *Draw, paint, sculpt, dance, etc. various dream images.*
While drawing a picture of the dream William associates his
dream to the biblical story of Jacob's ladder. William sees the
biblical association offering another perspective on his dream.
Jacob recognized that the place where he slept was sacred
although he wasn't originally aware of that. William sees this as
parallel to his own situation where he tends to see spirituality
and sex as opposed to each other rather than recognizing that
his body, sexuality and earthly existence are related to God and
are part of his spirituality.

In this section we have seen how the rules of dream interpretation work in a group setting. These rules can also be applied to individual or private dream interpretation *without* the
aid of a group. Many have found it valuable to explore their
dreams by applying these rules systematically when the group is
not available. Some dream group members have observed that
when they use this method in their individual work they imagine
the group around a table asking questions about each of the
dream images. To ask these questions *as if* in a seminar
stimulates their imagination and draws out different points of
view on the meaning of the images.

Notes

1. Please see introduction regarding extracurricular dream groups.
2. All of the names in the dream and of the seminar members have been changed to protect the confidentiality of the seminar. Also, the dialogue has been edited for length. The actual session took some two hours, rambled more, explored some interesting dead ends, etc. But the core is presented here.
3. Shadow is a term Jung used to denote all the "unpleasant qualities we like to hide together with the insufficiently developed functions and the contents of the personal unconscious." *Two Essays on Analytical Psychology, CW* 7, p. 66.
4. See William Irwin Thompson, *Blue Jade From the Morning Star: An Essay and a Cycle of Poems on Quetzlcoatl* (West Stockbridge, Mass., 1983), p. 10.

Conclusion

In this book we have seen the changing place and evaluation of dreams in religion and psychology. The history of dream interpretation shows that it was originally carried out within a religious context. It also shows a movement toward dreamers being the authority over the meaning of their own dreams and toward interpreting dreams outside the analytical and therapeutic context. Moving dream interpretation outside the clinical setting also encourages a return to the spiritual interpretation of dreams.

We also considered the broad outlines of psychology's contributions to dream interpretation. Experimental psychology's emphasis on physiological and quantitative measures limits its contribution to dream interpretation in the psychology of religion. The physiological studies of dreaming are especially interesting in comparing these REM states to meditation or trance states, but they shed little light on the *inner meaning* of dream states. Calvin Hall's quantitative analysis of dream content gets closer to the inner meaning of dreams and his methods offer exciting possibilities for comparing various religious dream symbols between different cultures and different religions.

Unfortunately Hall does not accept what William James described at the turn of the century: the subliminal region (the subconscious or the unconscious[1]) is an empirical phenomenon in psychology and it is also where we would expect the inbreaking of the divine. Hall states emphatically that dreams are not mysterious or supernatural phenomena. While we may grant that Hall's work makes dreams more accessible to large numbers in our secular culture, he overstates what is conclusively known about the realm of dream experience.

Freud's contribution to dream interpretation is foundational. He fashioned the essential method by which we arrive at the meaning of dreams, namely, the dreamer's personal associations to each element of the dream. All of the depth psychologies that try to get at the inner meaning of dreams use some form of personal association to dream symbols. Freud's terms "latent dream" and "manifest dream" are not particularly useful in the psychology of religion, especially when the latent dream (the meaning of the dream) is arrived at by a method that reduces potentially religious symbols to obsessional, wishful or regressive phenomena. While there is no doubt that such phenomena lie behind *some* religious dream symbols, there is no empirical justification for reducing all or even most dream symbols to pathological formations.

Humanistic psychology renders a more positive interpretation of religious symbols in both dream and waking experience. Abraham Maslow and Erich Fromm, for instance, both see that religious symbols are able to express the highest human values and potential. Perls' "hot seat" technique in Gestalt dream work frequently enables the dreamer to re-own religious dream symbols as cherished life values, untapped inspirations and a reverence for the mystery of human existence. When Gestalt work moves into these depths, it deals with basically religious concerns in terms of ethical values, the meaning of life and world-view. The drawback of humanistic psychology is its tendency to limit the interpretations of religious symbols to human potential. While this is an advance over experimental psychology's general neglect of religion and Freud's consistently negative evaluation of religion, it still restricts dream symbols primarily to the individual's psyche.

Of psychology's "four forces" the transpersonal approach seems to be the most effective for dealing with dream interpretation in the psychology of religion. It is a development of the central inspirations of William James, father of the psychology of religion. For James the concerns of empirical science and religion meet in the realm of the subconscious (or unconscious).

James saw that the vast uncharted and largely unknown territory of the subconscious is a region in common to both psychology and religion. In this region both recognize forces that influence yet transcend the individual person. Even from the brief overview of psychology in the second chapter it is clear that psychology is not a unified science with a single method. It might be more accurate to speak of the "psychological sciences" than the "science of psychology." We should also keep in mind the relationship between various psychological methods and the philosophical views that undergird these methods. Psychological methods are grounded in philosophical presuppositions which largely determine what will be observed and how that will be evaluated. There is no neutral ground here. A psychology can only *appear* to be without a philosophical foundation by being unaware of it or refusing to examine it.

Thus when we consider the major psychological methods of dream interpretation we note that certain philosophies and values associated with some of these approaches restrict the relevance they have to the psychology of religion. The conflict here is not due to scientific methods in psychology but rather to the underlying philosophy of a particular scientist or scientific school. For instance, when Calvin Hall asserts that dreams are not supernatural phenomena this is not simply a scientific conclusion based on empirical observation. Rather this view is part of his philosophy of life and his assumption that dreams present a picture of the dreamer's personality. We have examined this subjective hypothesis in chapter two and found it to be a very fruitful assumption in psychotherapy. But the effectiveness of one hypothesis (here, the subjective) does not automatically exclude other hypotheses such as the spiritual ones examined in chapter four.

An hypothesis is considered valid if it stands up to the verification principles of dream interpretation described in chapter four. Subjecting an interpretive hypothesis to verification merely tests the appropriateness of that hypothesis for a particular dream. It does not necessarily rule out other hypotheses even for the same dream. We observed in chapter four that the various dimensions of dreams are not mutually exclusive. The subjective interpretation of a dream does not necessarily exclude an objective interpretation of the same dream. Both may conform to standards of verification. So when Hall states that dreams provide a portrait of the dreamer's personality, he is correct. This subjective hypothesis frequently, perhaps even in the majority of cases, does unlock the meaning of a dream. But when he assumes that the subjective hypothesis denies the validity of spiritual hypotheses he abandons scientific accuracy and expresses his personal philosophy. What he affirms about the subjective hypothesis is correct but what he denies about the spiritual hypotheses goes well beyond what is empirically demonstrated.

Freud's attitude toward the religious hypotheses illustrates this same reductionist tendency. While he recognizes the subjective and objective hypotheses and later devoted some attention to the telepathic dimension of dreams, he ignores the possibility of the spirit-world and divine dimensions. While Freud's critique of religion has had the effect of purging religion of some of its regressive and negative aspects, his exclusion of the spiritual dimensions of dreams is merely an assumption without empirical foundation. Given the nature of verification in dream interpretation, an hypothesis cannot simply be ruled out in principle. It must be tried out provisionally to determine if it illuminates a dream and resonates with the dreamer. This is the same procedure whereby Freud originally demonstrated the validity of the subjective and objective dimensions of dreams. Unfortunately he did not extend this method to the spiritual dimensions of dreams. Thus, like Hall, Freud's affirmative observations about dreams are accurate and well-grounded while his deprecatory attitude toward the religious dimensions are not based on the same empirical procedure.

I wish to stress here that the objection to reductionist tendencies in certain psychological approaches is *not on theological grounds but on scientific grounds*. Some psychologists express what is more akin to religious dogma than scientific method when they assert without empirical justification that religious experience in dreams is impossible. There is nothing wrong with psychologists expressing their personal philosophies or their negative attitude toward the possibility of religious experience but they should not promote their private philosophy as if it were simply the truth or the product of empirical science.

William James is an example of a psychologist who recognized the limits of both science and religion as well as the area they have in common. James formulated his ideas about the subconscious as an hypothesis that can reconcile religion with science:

> Let me then propose, as an hypothesis, that whatever it may be on its *farther* side, the "more" with which in religious experience we feel ourselves connected is on its *hither* side the subconscious continuation of our conscious life. Starting thus with a recognized psychological fact as our basis, we seem to preserve a contact with "science" which the ordinary theologian lacks.[2]

He hoped that the hypothesis of the subconscious would lead to a greater understanding of religious experience and a greater openness of psychology to religious experience.

James describes the subconscious as the larger background of consciousness which is composed of a wide variety of phenomena, such as memories, inhibitions as well as inspirations of genius.[3] According to James, "invasions" from the subconscious occur in certain religious experiences such as sudden conversion and sporadic mystical experience. Thus he sees the subconscious as the area in which both psychology and religion share an interest; the hypothesis of the subconscious recognizes that the conscious person is continuous with a wider self through which religious experiences may come.[4]

While James did not write much about dreams, his idea about the subconscious as a potential region of religious experience has a bearing on dream investigation in the psychology of religion. His attitude has influenced the method of dream interpretation described in this book. Divine and spirit-world phenomena may be experienced through the medium of the unconscious, that is, in dreams. At least there are no scientific grounds for eliminating this possibility which is strongly suggested in many powerful and uncanny dreams. The spiritual dimensions of dream reference and a religious interpretation of the dream series are concrete ways to test this possibility of "spiritual in-breaking" and are at the heart of dream interpretation in the psychology of religion. As Jung points out, if people really believe in God, they should be open to the possibility that God may speak through their dreams.

To summarize, dream interpretation in the psychology of religion is becoming more democratic, participatory, provisional and comprehensive. More *democratic* because it is not restricted to trained analysts and therapists. Dream interpretation is often effectively done in groups and by individuals outside the clinical setting. *Participatory* in that the dreamer must participate in discovering the meaning of his or her own dreams. The meaning of dreams does not derive from an external authority, analyst or therapist. *Provisional* because any perspective used to illuminate a dream is seen as one of many possibilities, as a tentative hypothesis. It is considered a valid hypothesis if it resonates with the dreamer. *Comprehensive* since the various therapeutic and spiritual dimensions of dream reference help the dreamer to keep an open mind about the many possible meanings of dreams.

I have tried to show where each of these characteristics originate in history and psychology and how they appear in the practice of dream interpretation. I hope this contributes to the understanding of dream interpretation in the psychology of religion. I also hope that you, the reader, try out some of the rules of dream interpretation on your own dreams in order to explore the spiritual territory in the land of dreams.

Notes

1. James preferred the term subconscious to unconscious, but the region he described is similar to what Freud and Jung termed the unconscious.
2. *Ibid.*, p. 386.
3. *The Varieties of Religious Experience* (New York, 1958), p. 386.
4. *Ibid.*, p. 388.

Selected Bibliography

Allport, G. *The Individual and His Religion*. New York, 1960.

Argyle, M. and Beit-Hallahmi, B. *The Social Psychology of Religion*. Boston, 1975.

Artemidorus Daldianus. *The Interpretation of Dreams*. Translated by R. White. Park Ridge, N.J., 1975.

Assagioli, R. *Psychosynthesis*. New York, 1965.

Autra, R. *L'Interprétation des rêves dans la tradition Africaine*. Paris, 1983.

Bachelard, G. *The Poetics of Reverie*. Translated by D. Russell. Boston, 1960.

Batson, C.D. and Ventis, W.L. *The Religious Experience: A Social Psychological Perspective*. New York, 1982.

Beguin, A. *L'Ame romantique et le rêve*. Paris, 1939.

Bianchi, E. "Teaching Religion Through Dreams," *CSR Bulletin* 10/1 (February, 1979), 5-8.

Blacker, T. *A Pilgrimage of Dreams*. London, 1973.

Bonime, W. *The Clinical Use of Dreams*. New York, 1962.

Boss, M. *I Dreamt Last Night* . . . New York, 1977.

Breger, L., Hunter, I., and Lane, R. *The Effect of Stress on Dreams*. New York, 1971.

Bro, H. *On Dreams*. New York, 1968.

Brown, J.A. *Freud and the Post-Freudians*. New York, 1977.

Brown, L.B. (ed.). *Advances in the Psychology of Religion*. Willowdale, Ontario, 1985.

Buechsenschuetz, B. *Traum und Traumdeutung im Alterthume*. Wiesbaden, 1967.

Campbell, J. (ed.). *Myths, Dreams and Religion*. New York, 1968.

Castaneda, C. *The Eagle's Gift*. New York, 1981.

_____. *The Fire From Within*. New York, 1985.

_____. *The Second Ring of Power*. New York, 1979.

Cartwright, R. *Night Life: Explorations in Dreaming*. Englewood Cliffs, N. J., 1977.

Cirlot, J.E. *A Dictionary of Symbols.* New York, 1962.

Delaney, G. *Living Your Dreams.* New York, 1979.

Devereux, G. *Reality and Dream.* New York, 1951.

Domhoff, W. *The Mystique of Dreams: A Search for Utopia Through Senoi Dream Theory.* Berkeley, 1985.

Dourley,J. *The Illness That We Are: A Jungian Critique of Christianity.* Toronto, 1984.

Downing, J., and Marmorstein, R. *Dreams and Nightmares.* New York, 1973.

Dunne, J.W. *An Experiment With Time.* London, 1934.

Ehrenwald, J. *The ESP Experience: A Psychiatric Validation.* New York, 1978.

_____. *New Dimensions of Deep Analysis.* New York, 1975.

Eisenbud, J. *Paranormal Foreknowledge: Problems and Perplexities.* New York, 1982.

Eliade, M. *Myths, Dreams and Mysteries.* New York, 1957.

Ellenberger, H. *The Discovery of the Unconscious.* New York, 1970.

Erikson, E. "The Dream Specimen in Psychoanalysis," *Journal of the American Psychoanalytic Association* 2 (1954), 5-56.

_____. *Childhood and Society.* New York, 1978.

_____. *Ghandi's Truth.* New York, 1969.

_____. "The Nature of Clinical Evidence," *Daedelus* 87 (Fall, 1958), 65-87.

_____. *Identity, Youth and Crisis.* New York, 1968.

_____. *Young Man Luther.* New York, 1962.

Faber, H. *Psychology of Religion.* London, 1976.

Faraday, A. *The Dream Game.* New York, 1974.

_____. *Dream Power.* New York, 1972.

Fingarette, H. *The Self in Transformation.* New York, 1963.

Fischer, C. *Der Traum in der Psychotherapie: Ein Vergleich Freud'scher und Jung'scher Patiententraueme.* Muenchen, 1978.

Fischer, C. ed. *Preconscious Stimulation in Dreams, Associations and Images.* New York, 1960.

Foulkes, D. *Children's Dreams: Longitudinal Studies.* New York, 1982.

_____. *A Grammer of Dreams.* New York, 1978.

Frenkle, N. *Der Traum, Die Neurose, Das Religioese Erlebnis.* Zuerich, 1974.

Freud, S. *The Standard Edition of the Complete Psychological Works of Sigmund Freud.* Translated and Edited by J. Strachey. London, 1981. Cited throughout as *SE.* Volumes cited in this work:

Vol. IV. *The Interpretation of Dreams*. (First Part).

Vol. VII. *Fragment of an Analysis of a Case of Hysteria*.

Vol. IX. "Obsessive Actions and Religious Practices."

Vol. XIII. *Totem and Taboo*.

Vol. XV. *Introductory Lectures on Psychoanalysis*.

Vol. XVIII. *Group Psychology and the Analysis of the Ego*.

Vol. XXI. *Civilization and Its Discontents*.

Vol. XXI. *The Future of an Illusion*.

Vol. XXII. *New Introductory Lectures on Psychoanalysis*.

Vol. XXIII. *Moses and Monotheism*.

French, T., and Fromm, E. *Dream Interpretation: A New Approach*. New York, 1964.

Fromm, E. *The Forgotten Language*. New York, 1957.

_____. *Psychoanalysis and Religion*. New Haven, 1950.

Garfield, P. *Creative Dreaming*. New York, 1974.

_____. *Pathway to Ecstasy: The Way of the Dream Mandala*. New York, 1979.

Garma. A. *The Psychoanalysis of Dreams*. New York, 1974.

Gollnick, J. "A Childhood Dream" in *Flesh as Transformation Symbol in the Theology of Anselm of Canterbury: Historical and Transpersonal Perspectives*. Lewiston, New York, 1985. Pp. 25-32.

Guntrip, H. *Psychoanalytic Theory, Therapy and the Self*. New York, 1973.

Hall, C. *The Meaning of Dreams*. New York, 1966.

Hall, C., and Domhoff, W. "The Dreams of Freud and Jung," *Psychology Today*, 2/1 (June, 1968), 42-45; 64-65.

Hall, C., and Lind, R. *Dreams, Life and Literature: A Study of Franz Kafka*. Chapel Hill, North Carolina, 1970.

Hall, C., and Nordby, V. *The Individual and His Dreams*. New York, 1972.

Hall, J. *Clinical Uses of Dreams: Jungian Interpretations and Enactments*. New York, 1977.

_____. *Jungian Dream Interpretation*. Toronto, 1983.

Hartmann, E. *The Biology of Dreaming*. Springfield, Illinois, 1967.

Heisig, J. *Imago Dei: Jung's Psychology of Religion*. Lewisburg, Pa., 1979.

Hillman, J. *The Dream and the Underworld*. New York, 1979.

Horney, K. *Self Analysis*. New York, 1968.

James, W. *The Principles of Psychology*. Vol. II. Cambridge, Mass., 1981.

_____. "A Suggestion about Mysticism," *Journal of Philosophy*,

Psychology and Scientific Methods 7 (1910), 85-92.

_____. *The Varieties of Religious Experience.* New York, 1958.

Jenks, K. *Journey of a Dream Animal.* New York, 1975.

Johnson, R. *Inner Work: Using Dreams and Active Imagination for Personal Growth.* New York, 1986.

Jones, R. *The Dream Poet.* Cambridge, Mass., 1979.

_____. *The New Psychology of Dreaming.* New York, 1978.

Jung, C. *The Collected Works of C.G. Jung.* Edited by H. Read, M. Fordham and G. Adler. Translated by R. Hull. Princeton, 1953-1979. Cited throughout as *CW.* Volumes cited in this work:

Vol. 5. *Symbols of Transformation.* 1967.

Vol. 7. *Two Essays on Analytical Psychology.* 1966.

Vol. 8. *The Structure and Dynamics of the Psyche.* 1969.

Vol. 11. *Psychology and Religion: West and East.* 1969.

Vol. 12. *Psychology and Alchemy.* 1968.

Vol. 16. *The Practice of Psychotherapy.* 1966.

Vol. 18. *The Symbolic Life: Miscellaneous Writings.* 1980.

_____. *Dream Analysis: Notes of the Seminar Given in 1928-1930 by C.G. Jung.* Edited by W. McGuire. Princeton, 1984.

_____. *Memories, Dreams, Reflections.* New York, 1965.

_____. *The Visions Seminars.* Vols. I and II. Zuerich, 1976.

Keen, S. *Visions and Voices.* New York, 1970.

Kelsey, M. *God, Dreams and Revelation.* Minneapolis, 1974.

_____. *Dreams: A Way to Listen to God.* New York, 1978.

Kernberg, O. *Object Relations Theory and Clinical Psychoanalysis.* New York, 1976.

Knapp, B. *Dream and Image.* New York, 1976.

Koestler, A. *The Act of Creation.* London, 1969.

Kohut, H. *The Nature of the Psychoanalytic Cure.* Chicago, 1984.

_____. *The Restoration of the Self.* New York, 1977.

_____. *Self Psychology and the Humanities.* New York, 1985.

Kramer, M., and Winget, C. *Dimensions of Dreams.* Gainesville, Florida, 1979.

Kramer, M., (ed.). *Dream Psychology and the New Biology of Dreaming.* Springfield, Illinois, 1969.

LaBerge, S. *Lucid Dreaming.* New York, 1986.

Layard, J. *The Lady of the Hare: A Study in the Healing Power of Dreams.* London, 1977.

Lee, S., and Mayes, A. *Dreams and Dreaming.* Middlesex, Eng., 1973.

Lincoln, J. *The Dream in Primitive Cultures.* Baltimore, 1935.

MacKenzie, N. *Dreams and Dreaming.* New York, 1965.

Mahoney, M. *The Meaning in Dreams and Dreaming.* New York, 1966.

Malony, N. *Current Perspectives in the Psychology of Religion.* Grand Rapids, 1977.

Maslow, A. *The Farther Reaches of Human Nature.* New York, 1971.

_____. *Religion, Values and Peak-Experiences.* New York, 1969.

_____. *Toward a Psychology of Being.* Princeton, New Jersey, 1962.

Mattoon, M. *Applied Dream Analysis.* Washington, D.C., 1978.

May, R., and Caligor, L. *Dreams and Symbols: Man's Unconscious Language.* NewYork, 1968.

McCaffrey, P. *Freud and Dora: The Artful Dream.* New Brunswick, N.J., 1984.

McDargh, J. *Psychoanalytic Object Relations Theory and the Study of Religion.* London, 1983.

McLeester, D. *Welcome to the Magic Theater.* Amherst, Mass., 1977.

McLeod, S. *Dreams: A Portrait of the Psyche.* Saratoga, California, 1981.

Meier, C. *Die Bedeutung des Traumes.* Freiburg im Breisgau, 1972.

Mindell, A. *Dreambody.* Boston, 1982.

Moss, C.S. *The Hypnotic Investigation of Dreams.* New York, 1967.

Natterson, J., and Gordon, B. *The Sexual Dream.* New York, 1977.

Oates, W. *The Psychology of Religion.* Waco, Texas, 1973.

O'Flaherty, W. *Dreams, Illusions and Other Realities.* Chicago, 1984.

Oldham, J., Key, T., and Starak, I. *Risking Being Alive.* Victoria, Australia, 1978.

O'Nell, C. *Dreams, Culture and the Individual.* San Francisco, 1976.

Ornstein, R. *The Psychology of Consciousness.* Middlesex, Eng., 1982.

Oswald, I. *Sleeping and Waking.* Baltimore, Md., 1962.

Perls, F. *Ego Hunger and Aggression.* New York, 1969.

_____. *The Gestalt Approach and Eyewitness to Therapy.* New York, 1951.

_____. *Gestalt Therapy Verbatim.* Moab, Utah, 1974.

Perls, F., Hefferline, R., and Goodman, P. *Gestalt Therapy: Excitement and Growth in the Human Personality.* New York, 1951.

Piaget, J. *Play, Dreams and Imitation in Childhood.* New York, 1962.

Progoff, I. *At a Journal Workshop.* New York, 1975.

Pruyser, P. *A Dynamic Psychology of Religion.* New York, 1968.

Rainey, R. *Freud as Student of Religion: Perspectives on the*

Background and Development of His Thought. Missoula, Montana, 1975.

Rhyne, J. "The Gestalt Art Experience," in *Gestalt Therapy Now.* Edited by J. Fagan and I Shepherd. New York, 1970.

Rivers, W.H. *Conflict and Dream.* New York, 1923.

Rizzuto, A. *The Birth of the Living God: A Psychoanalytic Study.* Chicago, 1979.

Rossi, E. *Dreams and the Growth of Personality.* New York, 1972.

Ruitenbeek, H. (ed.). *Heirs to Freud.* Brattleboro, Vermont, 1967.

Rycroft, C. *The Innocence of Dreams.* London, 1979.

Sanford, J. *Dreams: God's Forgotten Language.* Philadelphia, 1968.

Savary, L., Berne, P., and Williams, S. *Dreams and Spiritual Growth.* New York, 1984.

Scott, C. (ed.). "Approaches to Dreaming: An Encounter with Medard Boss," *Soundings* 60/3 (Fall, 1977).

Sechrist, E. *Dreams: Your Magic Mirror.* New York, 1968.

Sharma, J. and Siegel, L. *Dream-Symbolism in the Sramanic Tradition.* Calcutta, 1980.

Sharpe, E. *Dream Analysis.* New York, 1978.

Sime, J. *The Land of Dreams.* Toronto, 1944.

Singer, Jerome. *The Inner World of Daydreaming.* New York, 1975.

Singer, June. *Boundaries of the Soul.* Garden City, N.J., 1973.

Sparrow, G. *Lucid Dreaming.* Virginia Beach, Va., 1976.

Spilka, B., Hood, R. and Gorsuch, R. *The Psychology of Religion: An Empirical Approach.* Englewood Cliffs, New Jersey, 1985.

Starak, I. "Rosnerian Gestalt: Reconceptualizing Gestalt Therapy." Unpublished paper presented at the Fifth Australian Conference on Family Psychotherapy in Canberra, September, 1984.

Stein, M. (ed.). *Jungian Analysis.* LaSalle, Illinois, 1982.

_____. *Jung's Treatment of Christianity.* Wilmette, Illinois, 1985.

Stekel, W. *Sex and Dreams: The Language of Dreams.* Boston, 1922.

Strunk, O. (ed.). *The Psychology of Religion: Historical and Interpretive Readings.* Nashville, 1971.

Sullivan, H.S. *The Interpersonal Theory of Psychiatry.* New York, 1953.

Sutich, A. "Introduction," *Journal of Humanistic Psychology,* 1/1 (1961), vi-ix.

_____. "Statement of Purpose," *Journal of Transpersonal Psychology,* 1/1 (1969), i.

Tart, C. *Altered States of Consciousness.* Garden City, N.J., 1972.

_____. *Transpersonal Psychologies.* New York, 1975.

Tisdale, J. *Growing Edges in the Psychology of Religion*. Chicago, 1980.

Ulanov, A. *Picturing God*. Cambridge, Mass., 1986.

———. and Ulanov, B. *Religion and the Unconscious*. Philadelphia, 1975.

Ullman, M., Krippner, S., and Vaughan, A. *Dream Telepathy*. New York, 1973.

Ullman, M., and Zimmerman, N. *Working With Dreams*. New York, 1979.

Van Dusen, W. *The Natural Depth in Man*. New York, 1972.

Von Grunebaum, E. and Caillois, R. *The Dream and Human Societies*. Berkeley, 1966.

Von Uslar, D. *Psychologie der Religion*. Zuerich, 1978.

Watkins, M. *Waking Dreams*. New York, 1977.

White, V. *God and the Unconscious*. Cleveland, 1961.

———. *Soul and Psyche*. London, 1960.

Wilber, K. *The Atman Project*. Wheaton, Illinois, 1982.

———. *A Sociable God*. New York, 1983.

Williams, S. *Jungian-Senoi Dreamwork Manual*. Berkeley, 1980.

Witkin, H. and Lewis, H. *Experimental Studies of Dreaming*. New York, 1967.

Wolff, W. *The Dream: Mirror of Conscience*. Westport, Conn., 1952.

Wolman, B. (ed.). *Handbook of Dreams: Research, Theories and Applications*. New York, 1979.

Woods, R. and Greenhouse, H. *The New World of Dreams*. New York, 1974.

Name Index

Aesculapius, 16
Allport, G., 101-102
Aquinas (St. Thomas), 20
Argyle, M., 118 (note)
Aristotle, 19, 142 (note)
Aserinsky, E., 39
Assagioli, R., 37, 114-117
Batson, D., 119 (note)
Baudelaire, C., 21
Binswanger, L., 58
Boss, M., 58
Brown, L.B., 118 (note), 119 (note)
Carus, C.G., 20
Cicero, 19
Clark, W.H., 119 (note)
Deikman, A., 120 (note)
Delaney, G., 32
Domhoff, W., 46 (note)
Dora's dream, 53-56
Dourley, J., 111
Ehrenwald, J., 144 (note)
Eliade, M., 143 (note)
Erikson, E., 23, 94-95
Faber, H., 118 (note)
Faraday, A., 23-24, 141 (note)
Fingarette, H., 95
Freud, S., 21-22, 38, 48-56, 92-93,
    97, 134, 166
Freud's dreams, 43-45
Fromm, E., 23, 103-108, 166
Galen, 142 (note)
Garfield, P., 31-32
Hall, C., 41-45, 91, 165
Hall, J., 110
Happich, C., 116-117

Heidegger, M., 58
Hermes, 150
Hippocrates, 141 (note)
Hirai, T., 120 (note)
Hoffmann, E.T., 21
Hugo, V., 21
Jacob, 158, 162
James, W., 67-68, 79-87, 95, 169
Jerome (St.), 29
Johnson, R., 30-31
Jung, C.G., 23, 67, 68-74, 104-108,
    111-114, 134, 142-143 (note)
Jung's dreams, 43-45
Kasamatsu, A., 120 (note)
Kelsey, M., 20, 29-30, 142 (note)
Kleitman, N., 39
Kohut, H., 96-97
LaBerge, S., 88-91
Makhir, 137
Malony, N., 118 (note)
Maslow, A., 37, 67, 98-101, 166
McCaffrey, P., 57 (note)
McDargh, J., 96
McLeester, D., 27
Mercury, 150
Meyers, F., 142 (note)
Mohammed, 18
Moritz, K., 20
Nerval, G., 21
Nodier, C., 21
Novalis, 20
Oates, W., 118 (note)
Perls, F., 59-64, 108, 134, 141
    (note), 166
Quetzlcoatl, 150

179

Subject Index

181

Studies in the Psychology of Religion

Date Due.